Notes from the Boundless Frontier

By Edward Esko

One Peaceful World Press
Becket, Massachusetts

Published by One Peaceful World, Becket, Massachusetts, U.S.A.

For further information on mail-order sales, wholesale or retail
discounts, distribution, translations, and foreign rights, please
contact the publisher:

One Peaceful World Press
P.O. Box 10
308 Leland Road
Becket, MA 01223
U.S.A.

Telephone (413) 623-2322
Fax (413) 623-8827

First Edition: September 1992
10 9 8 7 6 5 4 3 2 1

ISBN 0-9628528-8-0
Printed in U.S.A.

Contents

Macrobiotica

The way of health and happiness.

Yin, yang in harmony

With life and nature guiding us.

Self-reflection and transformation.

Living with an endless dream.

One grain, ten-thousand grains

With gratitude eternally.

**--Sung to the Ode to Joy chorus
of Beethoven's Ninth Symphony**

Introduction

When I sat down to my first meal of brown rice and vegetables more than twenty years ago, I knew I was entering a new world. Through macrobiotics, I would discover how to live in harmony with nature, and how to realize health and peace in daily life. I would learn how to see the human and natural worlds, including my own life, as a reflection of the endless order of change. The philosophy of macrobiotics would ultimately reveal the key to life's most basic questions, and on a social level, provide many opportunites to share the universal dream of health and peace with people in all corners of the globe.

The writings in this book are a reflection of my thoughts and experiences over the past twenty years. They were inspired by the many teachers and friends I have met and studied with, especially Michio and Aveline Kushi, Lima Ohsawa, William Dufty, Herman and Cornelia Aihara, Clim Yoshime, Shizuko Yamamoto, and my colleagues at the Kushi Institute and other macrobiotic centers around the world. Some of these articles were published in *Order of the Universe*, the *One Peaceful World Newsletter*, *Macrobiotics Today*, and *MacroNews*, and some are being published here for the first time. The idea of putting my essays into a book was inspired by George Ohsawa, the founder of modern macrobiotics, who wrote many fascinating articles and books on the application of macrobiotic principles.

I would like to thank everyone who helped make this book a reality. I would especially like to thank my parents, Edward and Elizabeth Esko, my wife Wendy, and our children, Eric, Mark, Daniel, Thomas, Julia, Matthew, and Amanda, for their support and encouragement. I thank Alex Jack, of One Peaceful

World Press, for guidance in completing this project, and Gale Jack for copyediting the manuscript. I thank Bob Ligon and Carl Ferre of the George Ohsawa Macrobiotic Foundation for encouraging the writing of this book, and for their helpful suggestions. I thank Lisa Cloutier and George Wiel for help with typing and production, Carry Wolf and Ulrike Hansen for their support, and Rich Meyers for help with proofreading. I would also like to thank Bettina Zumdick for contributing the wonderful drawings, and Liliane Papin for the delightful photos of Japan.

Throughout history, the image of the frontier has inspired countless generations of humanity. From Columbus's discovery of the New World five-hundred years ago, to the American Frontier of the last century, to President Kennedy's New Frontier of a generation ago, the possibility of extending the boundaries of human experience has always excited the human spirit. Now, at the beginning of a new millennium, the macrobiotic way of life is spreading rapidly around the globe. At this turning point in history, humanity is about to embark on its most incredible journey so far--a journey toward new frontiers of health, peace, and endless self-discovery.

Edward Esko
Becket, Mass.
June, 1992

Part I: Anecdotes and Experiences

1. John and Yoko in Boston

To me, John Lennon was the most interesting of the Beatles. He had a fantastic stage presence, a terrific rock 'n roll voice, and an uncanny knack for combining clever lyrics with innovative chord changes and melodies. He enjoyed doing what he was doing, had the courage to speak his mind (even when it got him into trouble), and was known and loved around the world.

John's songs seemed to define the experience of coming of age in the Sixties, from the exhilaration of falling in love *(I Wanna Hold Your Hand, I Should Have Known Better, Thank You Girl)*, to the experience of lost love *(Ticket to Ride, I'll Be Back, I Don't Want to Spoil the Party)*, to the search for inner meaning *(You've Got to Hide Your Love Away, In My Life, Help!)* to the development of social awareness and the quest for peace *(Revolution, All You Need is Love, Give Peace a Chance, Imagine)*. During the Sixties, he seemed to be at the cutting edge of everything. It was hard to tell whether John and the Beatles imitated life, or whether life was imitating John and the Beatles.

Like others of my generation, the Beatles inspired me to play the guitar and sing, and to write songs. My goal wasn't to be an accomplished musician; I wanted to express myself the way John Lennon did. Music provided an outlet for youthful energy and a means of putting across a message, regardless of what that message happened to be.

As the Sixties drew to a close, however, yang changed to yin. The Beatles, who had come together with such energy and conquered the whole world, eventually went their separate ways. Our lives changed as well. For me, macrobiotics replaced music as the focus of my life. However, I never lost my appreciation for the Beatles. When I moved to Boston in the early Seventies, I wrote articles for *East West Journal*, the monthly journal started by students of the Kushis. I did interviews with several well known personalities, one of whom was Yoko Ono. I travelled to New York early in 1973 to interview Yoko at the apartment she shared with John in Greenwich Village.

It was quite a shock when, one afternoon in 1976, Aveline Kushi called me at my office at the East West Foundation and said that John and Yoko were in Boston and were on their way to see Michio at the Kushi house. She asked if I would join them. I replied that I would be happy to, and rushed downstairs to catch the Riverside trolley to Brookline. Twenty minutes later, as I entered the front door of the Kushi house, Aveline was standing in the hallway. She pointed to the library and said in a soft voice, "John and Yoko are inside with Michio. Please go in." I opened the door. Michio was sitting between John and Yoko on a sofa at the other end of the room. From what I could tell, Michio seemed to be answering their questions about diet.

As the conversation drew to a close, John and Yoko stood up and started walking in my direction. I offered them my hand and introduced myself. Yoko said, "You're the fellow who did the interview in the *East West Journal*. John and I enjoyed it very much." Then John added that the *Journal* was now his favorite magazine.

At that moment the library door opened and Aveline entered. She and Michio said a few words to Yoko in Japanese, and invited the Lennons to take seats at a large table at the other end of the library. Aveline mentioned that the Seventh Inn, the macrobiotic restaurant in Boston, was preparing a special dinner, and that food would be arriving soon. Both John and Yoko said that that sounded wonderful, and they would be delighted to stay for dinner. By this time, Wendy had come into the room and she and I took seats next to the Lennons. Michio and Aveline excused themselves and left the room.

John was completely down to earth and unpretentious. He was a witty conversationalist. Because we had grown up with his music and followed his adventures for years, it felt like we were talking with an old friend. I asked him about the other Beatles and whether he still had contact with them. I asked if they were also interested in macrobiotics or had developed some type of dietary awareness. John replied that George Harrison and Paul McCartney were both vegetarian, and said that the other Beatles were like old high school chums. He had shared many interesting adventures with them, but like classmates who separate at graduation, each of the Beatles were pursuing their own interests. He added that he did talk with the other Beatles on occasion and still felt close to them.

Then the subject turned to macrobiotics. John mentioned that he first read Ohsawa years before, and that Ohsawa's writings had had a profound effect on his life and thinking. "Ohsawa was truly incredible," he said. He added that he and Yoko were friends with William Dufty and Gloria Swanson, and were frequent dinner guests at Gloria's New York apartment. *Sugar Blues* had just come out, and John said he felt it was the most important book of the decade.

We also talked about food. John mentioned that he had recently stopped coffee. He thought that drinking coffee was hard on the kidneys and said he felt better and stronger without it.

By this time, a crowd had materialized in the hallway, seemingly out of nowhere. The food from the restaurant arrived, and Michio, Aveline, and other guests joined us at the table. The conversation continued over dinner, with John and Yoko serving as the focus of a lively and animated discussion. Following dinner, John and Yoko mingled with the crowd, which by this time had grown quite large. Some people had come to say hello, others brought cameras and took pictures, and others simply came for a glimpse of John Lennon.

Walking out into the hallway, I noticed Michio and Aveline's youngest son, Hisao, sitting quietly by himself. That was unlike Hisao, who was normally very talkative. Hisao was a dedicated Beatles fan, as were all the Kushi children. They had a large collection of Beatles records and often played Beatles songs on the guitar and piano. Hisao, who was about ten at the time, was the only one of the Kushi children at home that day. The others were away at school or traveling. It seemed that the shock of seeing John Lennon right here, *having dinner in his house*, had caused Hisao to become uncharacteristically shy and at a loss for words.

Fortunately, Michio understood Hisao's dilemma and came to his rescue. The moment was quite unforgettable. John was seated on a sofa in the library, and Michio came through the door leading Hisao by the hand and holding a camera in the other. He said something to the effect that Hisao was a big fan of the Beatles, and asked John if he would mind being in a picture with Hisao. John smiled and said "of course," and Michio guided Hisao to the sofa next to John. He then took a position in front of them, focused the camera, and snapped the picture. Everyone laughed. As soon as the photo session was complete, Hisao slipped out of the room, grinning from ear to ear.

As the evening drew on, the crowd eventually thinned. I remembered John's earlier remark that the *East West Journal* had become his favorite magazine. I had a complete collection of *Journals* stored in a closet upstairs and thought they would make a nice gift for John and Yoko. I went upstairs, dug through the closet, and came downstairs with the stack of *Journals* under my arm. As John and Yoko were getting ready to leave, I said to John, "Here is a complete set of *East West Journals*. I would like you to have them." John smiled and said, "Thank you very much Edward. I'm sure we'll enjoy them." With that I handed the magazines to John and he placed them in the back of the van parked in front of the house.

Michio and Aveline said goodbye to John and Yoko in both Western and Eastern fashion, first shaking hands and then bowing. As John and Yoko got into the van, all of us stood on the front porch waving and saying goodbye. It had been a memorable evening. As they drove off, the words to *Imagine*, John's anthem for world peace, drifted into my mind. I realized that in his life and his art, John Lennon was a pioneer who shared our dream of one peaceful world.

2. Dietary Goals for the United States

In 1977, the U.S. Senate came out with *Dietary Goals for the United States*. This landmark report summarized evidence linking the modern diet with cancer, heart disease, and other chronic illnesses, and advised Americans to make dietary changes in the direction of macrobiotics. *Dietary Goals* energized the Boston macrobiotic community, and changed forever the concept of nutrition in America. It was followed by dozens of official reports that echoed its conclusions.

In the Foreword to *Dietary Goals*, Senator George McGovern stated:

"The purpose of this report is to point out that the eating patterns of this century represent as critical a public health concern as any now before us. We must acknowledge and recognize that the public is confused about what to eat to maximize health. If we as a government want to reduce health costs and maximize the quality of life for all Americans, we have an obligation to provide practical guides to the individual consumer as well as set national dietary goals for the country as a whole. Such an effort is long over-due. Hopefully, this study will be a first major step in that direction."

One of the people who played a crucial role in the evolution of *Dietary Goals* was a doctor named Mark Hegsted. At that time, Dr. Hegsted was with the Department of Nutrition at the Harvard School of Public Health. In a statement before the Senate Select Committee on Nutrition and Human Needs, chaired by George McGovern, and later published in *Dietary Goals*, Dr. Hegsted said:

"It should be emphasized that this diet (high in saturated fat, sugar, and cholesterol) which affluent people generally consume is everywhere associated with a similar disease pattern—high rates of heart disease, certain forms of cancer, diabetes, and obesity. These are the major causes of death and disability in the United States. The risks associated with eating this diet are demonstrably large. The question to be asked therefore, is not why should we change our diet but why not? What are the risks associated with eating less meat, less fat, less cholesterol, less sugar, less salt, and more fruits, vegetables, unsaturated fats and cereal products—especially whole grain cereals. There are none that can be identified and important benefits can be expected."

In the autumn of 1977 I called on Dr. Hegsted at Harvard. I presented case histories and other documentation, and outlined the macrobiotic diet. I pointed out how macrobiotics was in many ways similar to the recommendations in *Dietary Goals*. Dr. Hegsted expressed genuine appreciation for the contribution being made by macrobiotic education, and said that he had recently come under fire from the food industry, especially the meat and sugar industries, as well as from some members of the medical profession, for his statements in *Dietary Goals*.

An amazing coincidence occurred that morning. In the middle of our discussion, Dr. Hegsted announced that Dr. Gio B. Gori of the National Cancer Institute was about to arrive for a meeting. Dr. Gori had addressed the Senate Nutrition Committee the year before and stated that scientific evidence pointed to an unmistakable connection between diet and cancer. Dr. Gori even went so far as to state that diet could be the single most important factor in causing cancer. His statement was carried on national television and received a great deal of attention in the press.

When Dr. Gori arrived, Dr. Hegsted invited him to join our discussion. At one point, both men asked about the the theoretical basis of the macrobiotic diet, and I explained the concept of yin and yang, referring to it as a "dialectical" classification of food. I used as examples such things as the complementary-antagonism existing between animal and vegetable foods, sodium and potassium, saturated and unsaturated fat, simple and complex sugars, and temperate and tropical species of plants and animals.

Both men listened intently. Dr. Hegsted agreed that the macrobiotic diet was nutritionally sound, but found the "dialectical" classification of food difficult to understand. He remarked that he would probably have trouble explaining it to his colleagues. Dr. Gori added that he basically agreed with the macrobiotic idea, but because of his official position, he was not able to speak as freely about diet as he would like to. Nevertheless, he acknowledged the contribution that macrobiotic education had made to furthering nutrition awareness in America, and encouraged everyone in the macrobiotic movement to continue their valuable work.

Soon afterward, I invited Dr. Hegsted to join Michio Kushi and me for lunch at a macrobiotic restaurant. Dr. Hegsted found the macrobiotic dishes quite delicious. Michio thanked him for taking a courageous public stand on issues of vital importance in the face of strong opposition. As the meeting drew to a close, Dr. Hegsted offered to help our efforts in any way he could.

Over the last three decades, macrobiotics has played a pivotal role in changing public awareness about diet and health. The natural food movement, which macrobiotic educators had started in the Sixties, eventually blossomed into the health revolution of the Seventies and Eighties. Leading medical research institutions began to give serious consideration to the role of diet in cancer, heart disease, and other chronic illnesses, and started recommending a naturally balanced diet along the lines of macrobiotics as a means of preventing these illnesses. Even such traditionally conservative organizations as the American Medical Association and the American Cancer Society began to consider the importance of diet. As a 1978 article in the *Community Nutrition Institute Newsletter* stated:

"The American Cancer Society, which for years has fought a battle against cigarette smoking, may launch a similar campaign against foods suspected of causing cancer. Frank J. Rauscher, senior vice president of research and a former director of the National Cancer Institute, told a recent press conference that excess beef consumption might be a target, along with high-fat foods and meats cured with sodium nitrite. Rauscher noted that some studies have linked high-fat diets to breast cancer in women and colon cancer in men. 'It's premature now,' he said, 'but I think we're getting close to a point where we'll have to mount a campaign against improper diets that may cause cancer.'"

****

Macrobiotic Dietary Guidelines

Increase intake of:	*Decrease intake of:*
Complex carbohydrates	Simple sugars
Vegetable proteins	Animal proteins
Low-fat foods	High-fat foods
Low or no-cholesterol foods	High-cholesterol foods
Organically grown foods	Foods that have been chemically sprayed or fertilized
Naturally processed foods	Artificial or chemically processed foods
Whole foods	Refined and partial foods
Foods rich in fiber	Foods that have been devitalized

3. Images of Japan

I left Boston for San Francisco early in September, 1978. After spending a week in the Bay Area, I boarded a Japan Airlines flight for Tokyo. Twelve hours later, I arrived at the Tokyo International Airport at Narita. The airport is about an hour by bus from the city, and after a short ride, I was met by Eiji Kohso, a friend from Nihon CI (Japan Center Ignoramus), the macrobiotic center in Tokyo.

My first week in Japan was spent in Tokyo as the guest of friends at Nihon CI. Activities that week included a tour of the center's multi-storied facility in a quiet section of the city, participation in several cooking classes, including one given by Lima Ohsawa, and presentation of a report on macrobiotics in America at a conference on alternative medicine.

After the week in Tokyo, I boarded the Shinkansen (bullet-train) for Kyoto, and was met at the Kyoto station by Michel Matsuda, who with several of his brothers and their wives, managed a small macrobiotic center. Michel started macrobiotics in the early 1960s. He was given the name Michel by George Ohsawa. I had met Michel in 1973 in Boston. He spent almost a year in Boston then, studying English, working at the Erewhon warehouse on Farnsworth street (Erewhon was the natural food company started by the Kushis), and attending Michio's seminars in the evenings. For six months, he and I were roommates at the University Road study house in Brookline, near Boston.

With the help of Michel and my friend Mr. Kazama of Mitoku, the company that distributes high-quality macrobiotic

17

products throughout the world, I managed to find a house in the Uzumasa section of the city. Uzumasa is located on the outskirts of the city, and is surrounded by rice fields and beautiful mountains. It is well-known throughout Japan as the home of Koriuji, the temple that contains the wooden statue of Miroku Bosatsu (the Buddha of the Future), carved over a thousand years ago out of a single block of wood. This magnificent work of Buddhist art is one of Japan's most prized national treasures.

Adapting to A New Environment

Wendy arrived in Japan in October, accompanied by our two children, Eric, age four, and Mark, age one-and-a-half. I met them at Narita, and on the following day, we boarded a plane for Osaka, which is about an hour by car from Kyoto. The flight offered a fantastic view of Mt. Fuji.

In preparation for their arrival, I had begun to arrange several jobs teaching English. With the help of friends, I began calling language institutes in Kyoto, and managed to arrange a teaching schedule that would generate enough income to pay the rent and keep rice in the pressure cooker. As I later discovered, teaching English offered wonderful opportunities to make new friends and become better acquainted with Japan.

Naturally, the arrival of a young American couple with two small children in this typical Kyoto neighborhood created a minor sensation. The kindness of our neighbors was overwhelming. Within days of our arrival, they began bringing furniture and other things for our use. These included a kotatsu (a small, low dining table with a built-in heater), a China cabinet, dishes, and other useful items.

Gradually, our neighbors began to notice that we were unlike most visitors to Japan. For one thing, our diet was very strange. They found it somewhat hard to believe that we ate brown rice, soba, natto, miso soup, and other foods that were considered old fashioned. Also, they probably thought it strange that our children had never had cow's milk, and did not eat the sugary snacks and candy at the corner store. After hearing that

18

both of the children had been breast-fed, one neighbor remarked, "You are like old-style Japanese!"

Many of the foods that we were used to eating in Boston were either not available, or were available but in a slightly different form. For example, whole grain bread is relatively unknown. Most supermarkets carry an unbleached white bread, and the toast served in restaurants is processed from bleached white flour. (It is also about two inches thick.) Muso, the macrobiotic food company in Osaka, distributed a form of yeasted whole grain bread, but the texture was somewhat different than whole grain breads in America or Europe. Generally speaking, baking has not become popular in Japan. Most houses don't have ovens, and the flour in Japan is not ideal for the types of breads and desserts we are used to in the West.

Living in Japan offered us an opportunity to eat rice that was grown nearby. During our stay, our consumption of rice increased tremendously, and we found the brown rice to be of very high quality. It was organically grown, and the grains were slightly smaller than American rices. It contained very few broken, chipped, or immature grains. Rice is still the principal food in Japan, but most people eat it in the form of white rice, or hakumai. Very few eat genmai, or brown rice. However, a growing number of people are starting to eat a form of partially refined rice that contains the hiaga, or bud, but does not contain the vitamin and mineral-rich outer coat.

Buckwheat, in the form of soba, is probably the next most popular grain. Whole buckwheat (kasha) is practically unknown, but the noodles in Japan were some of the best we have tasted. There are soba shops in practically every neighborhood where you can get a fairly high-quality bowl of noodles in broth, or noodles topped with tempura. Oats are practically unknown (or should I say "unused") in Japan, and we did not see any corn. Barley enjoys a very modest popularity, and millet, or awa, is mostly of the glutinous variety used in making mochi. It is very sweet and moist, and makes a delicious breakfast cereal.

The Ise Shrine

In December we had the opportunity to visit the Ise Shrine. We had heard about Ise in Michio's lectures in Boston, and friends who had been to Japan told us how special it was. In preparation for our visit, we found ourselves automatically eliminating various minor excesses from our diets, and eating more cleanly and simply. We were invited to visit the shrine by one of my English students, a young woman named Tamako Yamaguchi, whose parents lived in Mie Prefecture, not far from Ise.

The Ise Shrine consists of two main buildings: an Inner Shrine known as Kotaijingu or Naiku, an Outer Shrine known as Geku or Toyoukedaijingu, as well as more than 120 smaller shrines. The Inner Shrine is dedicated to Amaterasu-Omikami, the goddess of the sun, and the Outer Shrine is dedicated to Toyouke-Omikami, the goddess of agriculture, who presides over life-giving food, especially brown rice. The Shrine is one of the oldest, while at the same time one of the newest in Japan. It was first built nearly two-thousand years ago, and, incredibly enough, is rebuilt every twenty years according to the same plan. The structures are made entirely of cypress trees that give the buildings a rich, golden color, and each wooden column is placed directly in the soil. The roofs are thatched with a native grass called kaya, and at both ends of the roofs are two cross beams that project upward toward the heavens.

The town of Ise is to the south of Kyoto on the Pacific coast. In addition to the Shrine, it is also famous for its pearls. The three-hour train ride offered a panoramic view of the beautiful mountains and countryside of southern Japan.

Upon arriving at Ise, we boarded a small bus bound for the Shrine. On the road leading to the Shrine were many stone lanterns that bore the symbol of a chrysanthemum with sixteen petals. The chrysanthemum is also the symbol of the Imperial Family of Japan, and is used as the symbol of the Miroku Bosatsu, or Buddha of the Future. When you first arrive at the shrine grounds, you cross a wooden bridge that spans a small river known as the Isuzu. The bridge is rebuilt every twenty years along with the rest of the Shrine, and has two large wooden gates, or torii, at either end of it.

After crossing the bridge, we stopped at a small wooden structure at the center of which was a long stone basin filled with water from the river. The water is very clean and pure, and each person took one of the small wooden cups with long handles and scooped some of the water. The water was used to wash the hands, and in some cases, to wash out the mouth. We all felt more alert from the coolness of the water, and also felt cleansed.

The next stop, after passing through another huge wooden torii, was a small open area on the bank of the Isuzu. There were hundreds of beautiful carp in a variety of colors and sizes swimming close to the shore. The children naturally became very excited at the sight of these delightful fish.

As we approached the southern gate of Kotajingu, the Outer Shrine, we were struck by the many tall cryptomeria trees lining the walkway. Some are many centuries old, and reach over one-hundred feet. In such an environment, one begins to feel the energy of heaven and earth. Invariably, your posture straightens, and you become aware that you are a channel for these forces. That was similar to the feeling I experienced the previous October while walking through fields of ripening rice.

There are many things, both natural and manmade, in Japan that give one a sense of the energy flowing between heaven and earth. When I arrived in Tokyo, I attended a conference held in a modern steel and glass convention center in the Asakusa section of the city. Directly across the street from the convention center was the Meiji Shrine, at the center of which was a large pagoda. The pagoda towered into the air, and at the top of it was a long spiral pole that looked very much like an antenna. One could almost visualize the force of the universe spiraling down through the pole and along the pagoda's vertical spine.

The Ise Shrine gives one a sense of the purity of nature and the importance of living in harmony with it. After seeing it, we could understand that people in ancient times were living more or less macrobiotically. The Ise Shrine offered a glimpse of a very ancient cosmology and way of life based on harmony with nature.

Following our visit to Ise, we spent the night at the home of Tamako's parents deep in the mountains of Mie Prefecture. During the bus ride, we were treated to beautiful mountain scenery. In front of many houses were long wooden racks for drying daikon, some with hundreds of these long white roots drying in the December sun. Tamako's parents maintained many old traditions, and based their diet on the foods that grew in their vicinity. Her father was eighty-five at the time and went into the mountains every week to harvest shiitake. As Tamako said, "The mountains are his hobby; the mountains are his life."

During our stay in Mie, we had the opportunity to bathe in an old-fashioned Japanese bath heated by a wood fire. It was incredibly relaxing. After bidding farewell to our gracious hosts, we set out for Kyoto, feeling refreshed and renewed after this marvelous experience.

The Nara Daibutsu

Right after the week-long celebration of the New Year, Doug Johnson (a friend from Connecticut), my son Eric, and I went to the city of Nara to see the famous Daibutsu, or Great Buddha. Nara is located just to the south of Kyoto and is one of the ancient capitals of Japan. The capital was moved continuously northward over the last 1,500 years, from Ise in the south, to Nara, then to Kyoto in the 9th-century, and in the 1860s, to its present location in Tokyo.

The Daibutsu is housed in a temple known as Todaiji. Built during the Nara Period (around 752 A.D.), the temple is the headquarters of the Kegon sect of Buddhism. The temple is surrounded by parks through which deer roam freely. As we entered the temple complex, we were taken aback by the size of the building that houses the Daibutsu. Although it has been rebuilt several times because of fire, and is smaller than the original, it is still considered to be the largest wooden building in the world. It is a huge Oriental-style building with upper and lower sloping tile roofs and huge wooden columns. From a distance, it dwarfs the buildings around it. The building is in a large open area, and in front of it is a long, open walkway.

The scene inside the building had a surreal quality to it. The statue itself is gigantic: it is over fifty feet in height, and rests on an elevated platform. In front of the statue were several dozen monks in Buddhist robes, sitting in meditation and chanting. A huge table with food offerings and burning incense sat directly in front of the image. On either side of the Buddha were two Boddhisattvas, each over thirty feet in height, while the building itself was a sort of museum for Buddhist art, including calligraphy and statues. A continuous stream of people entered the building, lit incense in front of the image, and filed around the statue while looking at the various samples of art. The visitors, including many children, talked in hushed tones, and the chanting of the monks provided a muted undertone to their voices.

In my interpretation, the Daibutsu represents not the actual historical Buddha, but the infinite universe itself. By erecting such a massive building and bronze statue, the architects were attempting to convey a sense of infinite depth, breadth, and scope. The main statue most likely symbolizes infinity, while the Boddhisattvas to the left and right symbolize yin and yang, or the left and right hands of God. I admire greatly the skill of the architects and builders of this incredible structure, which conveys a sense of enormous size and depth in a way that no modern steel and glass structure can. The entire complex, including the building and surrounding area, is evidence of a wonderful intuitive grasp of yin and yang. The area around the building is very open and expansive, more yin, and the building itself is also yin—it is made entirely of wood and is very large. Counterbalancing this is the bronze image. Even though it is quite large, it is made of metal and has a very yang physiognomy—a very square face (with earlobes reaching to the shoulders) and it is sitting in a more yang, meditating posture in the center of the building.

As we left the temple grounds, I began to wonder why the builders of these shrines and temples chose the places they did for their creations. Suddenly the answer became clear. In those times, people were eating whole grains and vegetables, and were sensitive to the invisible currents of electromagnetic energy, or ki, that permeate nature. They obviously chose places with a particularly intense charge of energy to build their structures. For example, the city of Kyoto is surrounded by mountains that produce a powerful charge of energy. People in the past must have been sensitive to this since Kyoto contains more shrines and temples than anywhere else in Japan. The strong natural charge of energy in these places makes it much easier for those who visit to gain insight into the invisible spiritual world.

Traditional Versus Modern Diets

As with practically all modern nations, Japan is developing a large appetite for animal food. Once unheard of, dairy products are becoming increasingly popular among the Japanese. In the annual New Year's Eve program broadcast over NHK (the national television network), viewers were invited into different homes to see how people around the country were celebrating the holiday. One visit was with a family in the northern island of Hokkaido. Hokkaido is the main dairy farming area in Japan, with a climate similar to New England, and the family featured in the broadcast operated a large dairy farm there. Throughout Japan, viewers of this program were treated to scenes of cows and barnyards—perhaps for modern Japan, an appropriate way to begin the New Year.

Cheese, milk, butter, yogurt, and similar foods have all become a part of the average diet here. (Frozen pizza is also becoming popular.) As a result, since World War II, the size of Japanese children has increased steadily, and one sees many young people with poor complexions. Without doubt, the modern diet has invaded and is in the process of conquering Japan, and most likely the rest of Asia. (It is interesting to note that in order to restore the balance of trade, America has convinced the Japanese to expand their imports of two agricultural items: beef and oranges.)

When I lectured on macrobiotics at the Kyoto YMCA, many of the students were concerned about whether enough protein was available from a semi-vegetarian diet. I suggested that the idea that meat and dairy products are necessary for health was a modern fallacy, and that the Japanese shouldn't be so eager to replace their traditional common sense about food with modern ideas about nutrition. It wasn't until I explained how vegetable protein was superior to animal protein that they became more at ease with the idea. "We are a very scientific people," one woman said, and Wendy and I found ourselves in the curious position of trying to convince them that their traditional diet, based around grains and vegetables, was nutritionally superior to the modern Western diet.

Of course, the Japanese still consume far less animal food than do most Americans (about one-fifth as much meat), but it seems that consumption of meat is growing steadily, along with a corresponding rise in the consumption of sugar, milk, soft-drinks, and other extremely yin foods. The incidence of breast cancer, heart disease, and other degenerative diseases is also rising in Japan.

The YMCA Seminar

In January, 1979, we presented our first formal macrobiotic seminar in Japan. It was held at the Kyoto YMCA, located across the street from the Old Imperial Palace, and consisted of four Saturday afternoon sessions that included lectures and cooking classes. The classes were attended by about fifteen women, including teenagers and grandmothers. Many of the women already knew how to cook traditional Japanese foods and found the macrobiotic approach easy to understand. We especially enjoyed having one Obaasan (grandmother) in the class, since she would often comment, "That's the way we used to do it when I was growing up."

One of the students, a young English teacher named Keiko Takagi, wrote about the class: "I have been eating natural foods for the past few years and have been studying on my own, mainly through books and magazines. However, this was the first time I learned about the concept of yin and yang, and that animal protein is largely unnecessary. It was very surprising to learn that dairy products (even yogurt) are best avoided. Although some questions remain, I truly appreciate that the course has introduced me to valuable ideas and concepts hitherto unfamiliar to me."

A Visit to Kyozoin

In March, Michel Matsuda took us to Kyozoin, the Buddhist temple in Kyoto where George Ohsawa is buried. Kyozoin is a small but very beautiful temple in a very tranquil part of the city.

During the bus ride, we asked Michel about the meaning of the huge Chinese characters, or Kanji, cut into the sides of several of the mountains around the city. The characters represent the letter Dai or Tai, which means "large" or "great," and each is about a hundred meters long.

Michel explained that the characters are part of a week-long festival, known as O-Bon, held every August. The festival is Buddhist in origin, and is celebrated throughout the country. Its meaning is something like "return of the spirits," and it is believed that departed ancestors return from the spiritual world during the celebration in order to receive consolation and encouragement. During the festival, the huge symbols are set ablaze. This is done at night and is quite spectacular. The light from these fires is thought to guide the spirits on their journey to our world.

In Japan, the attitude that considers death as a continuation of life is a part of everyone's consciousness. This is combined with the awareness that an intimate relationship with departed ancestors should be maintained as a part of every family's daily life. At the spring and fall equinoxes, millions of people throughout the country visit the graves of their ancestors to offer prayers

26

and encouragement. These occasions are national holidays, as is the O-Bon festival.

Traditionally, no animal food is eaten during the week of O-Bon, and colorful festivities are held to send the spirits off on their return journey to the spiritual world. Throughout Japan, thousands of small paper boats, each carrying a tiny lit candle, are set afloat on rivers and allowed to drift out to sea.

Upon arriving at the temple, we bought a small bunch of flowers at the groundskeeper's house. Many people were at the temple that day, which is situated next to the headquarters of several large tea ceremony schools. On the way to the cemetery, we passed small, several-storied pagoda, and upon arriving at Mr. Ohsawa's grave, Michel put the flowers in their appropriate place, and poured water over the stone marker. Then Wendy, the children, and I took turns saying thank you to this man whom we never met but who has had a profound influence on our lives.

A Stone Chart of the Cosmos

Later that month, the four of us boarded the Shinkansen for Tokyo to visit the Kushi family. During our stay in Tokyo, Michio's father, Keizo, then in his eighties, invited us to look through the books in his library, which contained an extensive collection of works on many aspects of Japanese culture. He also explained the meaning of the wonderful stone lantern in the garden. Known as Ishi-no-Toro, the five-tiered lantern (which resembles a small pagoda), is actually a representation of Go-Gyo, or the five transformations of energy. It is, as he said, a small "chart of the cosmos."

The first tier of the lantern represents the metal energy, the most yang of these stages of change. The second, third and fourth tiers represent the energy of soil, water, and tree, respectively. The uppermost, or most yin tier represents the stage of fire energy. As Mr. Kushi explained, this cosmological design is why many pagodas have five stories.

Michio's brother, Masao, also explained the meaning of the Kushi family crest (which is now the logo of the Kushi Institute). In Japanese, it is known as Ken-Hanna-Bishi, or "sword-flower symbol." The symbol represents the balanced combination of yin (the flower) and yang (the sword). It is also the symbol of the Izumo Shrine on the western coast of Japan.

During our meeting, Kayoko, Masao's wife, served us mochi "Wakayama style." She explained that in Wakayama prefecture in southern Japan, mochi is often served in a broth of bancha tea. She placed several pieces of fresh brown rice mochi in a bowl and poured hot tea over it. She then brought in a small dish containing high quality sea salt, and added a pinch or two to the mochi. It was delicious.

It was during this meeting that the Kushis invited us to visit Wakayama to participate in a ceremony at Daitaiji, the Kushi family temple. Our visit to Wakayama proved to be one of the most memorable experiences we had in Japan.

Wakayama

On a fine Saturday morning in April, we boarded the train leaving Kyoto station for Osaka. From the main station in Osaka, we took the Osaka Loop Train to Tennoji station where we boarded the southbound train for Wakayama.

Much to our surprise, the train was packed. In fact, there were no seats, so for a while we made do by sitting on our travel bags. It wasn't until the train made several stops that we were able to find seats.

As we proceeded south, the crowded Kansai region gave way to beautiful countryside filled with scenic mountains. Here and there we could see flooded rice fields, and soon the ocean came into view. Eventually, the train stopped at a town called Kushimoto, where we could see many beautiful rock formations along the Pacific.

About five hours out of Osaka, we arrived at our destination—the stop known as Kii-Katsuura. We were met at the station by Michio's father, Keizo, and his brother, Masao.

28

Kii-Katsuura is an old fishing village that has recently become popular as a resort. After exchanging greetings, we boarded a small boat that was leaving for our hotel on the other side of the bay. The hotel is built alongside a mountain, and is well known for its hot spring. The spring is in a cave that opens onto the Pacific. Following a delicious dinner that featured an incredible array of fresh seafood, Wendy, the children, and I enjoyed a natural mineral bath in the spring. We all felt very relaxed and refreshed, and slept very well that night.

Daitaiji

After rising early the next morning, we went with Masao to an old whaling village not far from the hotel, where Daitaiji is located. The temple is situated in a beautiful wooded area. While walking through the temple and surrounding grounds, we discovered the meeting hall where Michio has lectured during his visits. After enjoying the wonderful surroundings for a while, we went to the nearby home of a family member to participate in the ceremony.

When we arrived, we found everyone sitting on zabutons; the room had a tatami (straw mat) floor, and opened onto a beautiful Japanese garden. A Buddhist priest entered and began the ceremony before a family shrine at the front of the room.

The ceremony consisted largely of chanting, which the priest performed at the shrine. Afterwards, everyone filed out of the house and up the path leading to the temple, behind which is a small cemetery where members of the Kushi family are buried. Each person placed incense on several of the the stone grave markers, while offering a short prayer. The priest took up a position near the front and continued chanting as the people filed past.

One month later, Michio and Aveline visited Kyoto, together with Lima Ohsawa, Gloria Swanson, and William Dufty. Wendy and I met them at Kyozoin in order to participate in a ceremony at George Ohsawa's grave. As in the ceremony at Wakayama, a

Buddhist priest from the temple chanted while each visitor offered prayers and placed lit incense on the stone marker.

Kumano

On the following day, Michio's father guided us on a tour of the area. Our first stop was the complex of shrines and temples known as Kumano, as well as the famous waterfall at Nachi, a beautiful stream of cascading water that drops several hundred feet straight down the side of a mountain. After touring Kumano, we took a drive through winding mountain roads until we arrived at the grounds of the Hongu Shrine. We walked through a huge torii (shrine gate) and up a stone stairway that led to the Shrine. The sky was a crystalline blue, and the late afternoon sun a warm yellow. The Shrine was surrounded by tall pine trees. As we were walking through these beautifully tranquil surroundings, Mr. Kushi remarked in English, "Sky is blue, trees are green, sun is bright—wonderful, isn't it?"

As we approached Hongu, we learned that it is at least as old as the Grand Shrine at Ise. Its four main buildings are dedicated to four great kami, or deities: Amaterasu-Omikami, the great heavenly shining goddess, represented by the sun and considered to be the guardian spirit of Japan; her elder brother, represented by the wind; and their parents, Izanami and Izanagi, who represent the primary forces of yin and yang. The simple elegance of these shrine buildings and surrounding grounds convinced us that their architects had a deep awareness of the order of the universe and man's place within it. Following our visit to Hongu, we returned to our hotel. Early the next morning we said goodbye to our kind hosts and boarded the train for Kyoto.

Saying Goodbye

At the end of May we returned to America. After bidding farewell to our friends and neighbors in Kyoto, we got into a taxi and drove to the international airport at Osaka, where we boarded a Korean Airlines flight bound for Honolulu and Los

Angeles. As the huge 747 turned out over the Pacific, Wendy and I reflected on our experiences in Japan. Our stay in Japan had offered us the chance to meet many wonderful and interesting people, as well as a rare glimpse of cultural traditions that are thousands of years old. Going to Japan strengthened our macrobiotic practice, and deepened our understanding of humanity, nature, and the boundless spiritual world. It also strengthened our desire to return to the West to teach and spread the macrobiotic way. With tears in our eyes, we said goodbye to this wonderful land and its people. Thank you Japan for letting us glimpse your ancient traditions while showing us many new possibilities for the future.

4. How *Recalled By Life* Happened

Coming back from Japan proved to be more difficult than we had anticipated. According to the Nine Star Ki, travel from West to East, or from Japan to America, was *Ankensatsu*, the most unfavorable direction for the year 1979. We had planned to return to the States in April. The trip to Wakayama described in the previous chapter had caused us to reschedule our return for the end of May. As it turned out, the time we had originally planned to return (initially to Philadelphia) was within days of the nuclear accident at Three Mile Island.

Another factor that added to the difficulty was our uncertainty about where to return to. In his most recent letter, Michio had suggested that we consider staying on the West Coast for a while. We had also written to Bill Tara and he had invited us to stay in London. Before we went to Japan, we had also considered moving to Washington, D. C. That was at the time of *Dietary Goals*, Michio's *Food Policy Recommendations for the United States*, and the somewhat heady feeling in the Boston community that the Carter Administration was open to macrobiotics, and that the United States was moving in a new dietary direction. After much deliberation, Wendy and I decided that we would try to restart the Washington, D. C. project. We could use my parents' home in Philadelphia as a base until we were able to locate a house in the Washington area.

That was our plan as we set out across the Pacific. However, once we arrived in Los Angeles, we started to have doubts. We both had an intuitive sense that it might be better to return to Boston. After a sleepless night in an airport hotel, we called friends in Boston and told them we would be arriving there on the following day. Our plan was to stay in a macrobiotic study house until we were able to sort things out.

Before leaving for Japan, we had spent several years developing educational programs in Boston. Our activities had included setting up the first Amherst Summer Program, arranging Michio's visits to Europe, and promoting awareness of the relationship between diet and cancer. These activities had included writing articles on macrobiotics and cancer, compiling case histories, editing publications, and setting up annual conferences on cancer and diet.

Upon returning to Boston, friends told us about about a doctor in Philadelphia who was the president of a hospital and who, through an unusual set of circumstances, had started macrobiotics because of prostate cancer. He seemed to be doing quite well. His name was Anthony Sattilaro. He had started to speak publicly about his experience and had many positive things to say about it. After hearing about Sattilaro's story, I encouraged friends at the East West Foundation to invite him to speak at the cancer and diet conference scheduled to take place that August in Boston.

In the meantime, our personal plans were still unclear. I was still attached to the idea of going to Washington, D. C., although friends in Boston were now encouraging us to stay there. After a great deal of soul-searching, we decided to proceed down the East Coast. Wendy and the two children would stay with my parents in Philadelphia while I went to Washington to look for a house to rent.

Our main contact in Washington was a friend named Tom Monte. I had spoken with Tom on several occasions before Japan. He was working as a reporter for a New Jersey newspaper and was preparing an article on macrobiotics. Upon returning to Boston, I had heard that Tom and his wife Toby had moved to Washington. He was working as an editor for *Nutrition Action*, the newsletter of the Center for Science in the Public Interest. I called Tom from Philadelphia and explained our situation. He graciously invited the four of us to stay at his home in Silver Spring, Maryland, while we were looking for a house in the area.

As it turned out, Tom's house was quite small, so Wendy, the two children, and I stayed downstairs on a small futon in the basement along with several cats. I would go out each day and visit real estate agencies looking for a suitable house. In the evening, I would return, join Wendy, the children, and the Montes for dinner, and then spend the evening discussing macrobiotics with Tom.

On one hot July evening, our conversation turned to the subject of macrobiotics and cancer. Jean Kohler's book, *Healing Miracles from Macrobiotics*, had just come out. I had helped the Kohlers edit the book before going to Japan. *Healing Miracles* chronicled Kohler's recovery from pancreatic cancer, and I mentioned to Tom my feeling that it would help our message reach a wide audience. During our conversation, an idea came to me: why not do an interview with Dr. Sattilaro for a popular magazine? I told Tom that he would be the perfect person to do an article on Dr. Sattilaro, and suggested that we submit it to a publication such as *Philadelphia Magazine* in order to reach a general audience. Tom agreed that an article about Dr. Sattilaro was a good idea, and we decided to call Sattilaro on the following day to present our idea.

The next day was a Sunday. As the day wore on, we decided to place the call. Tom dialed the number on the wall phone in the kitchen. Tom said, "Hello, Dr. Sattilaro? This is Tom Monte. I would like to talk to you about doing an article about your experience with macrobiotics. If you are interested, I can come to Philadelphia to meet with you about it." He then waited for Dr. Sattilaro's reply.

Dr. Sattilaro said, "Hello Tom. Thank you very much for calling. I've read several of your articles and thought they were terrific. I'd be happy to get together with you." Tom replied that they could start work on the article right away, and he would call back in several days to schedule a time to begin. Then he said, "I look forward to working with you. Thank you, good-bye." The whole conversation took about a minute.

Out of these first interviews came the story that was published in the March, 1980 *East West Journal*. The *Journal* story was picked up by the *Saturday Evening Post*, and eventually expanded into a book, *Recalled By Life*, published by Houghton-Mifflin. In the meantime, Wendy, the children, and I decided to return to Boston in order to set up a macrobiotic study house and teach at the Kushi Institute. As time went by, it became clear that the cancer and diet project we helped launch several years before was about to enter a new and more interesting dimension.

****

These accounts [of persons who recovered from cancer with the macrobiotic diet], are like the diaries of our Pilgrim forebears or the pioneers who settled the West. Traversing uncharted territory, often experiencing deep conflicts and divisions within their own households, and confronting skeptical and sometimes hostile powers, they pressed on, made many mistakes, and suffered agonizing personal and professional losses. But in the end, they came to a new awareness of themselves, the origins and causes of their illnesses, and the opportunity of helping others. They transformed their illnesses into health, their ignorance into understanding, and their fear into faith.

Alex Jack
from the Foreword to *Cancer-Free*

35

5. Buenos Aires

The trip to Buenos Aires took a full twenty-four hours. The flight began in Boston, included a stopover in New York, a nine-hour journey to Rio, a stopover at the Rio airport, and a two-and-a-half hour flight to Buenos Aires. There were plenty of empty seats on the long Pan Am flight to Rio, and as it was an overnight flight, I stretched out and tried to get some sleep. I had the feeling it was going to be a long trip.

I woke up several hours later. There was daylight outside the window. We were over the Amazon. Looking down, I saw a huge brown expanse through which rivers were running. Heat seemed to be rising from the earth. As we crossed the equator, I felt a strange sensation; something like a magnetic realignment. It felt as if the plane had turned around and was heading back toward the Pole rather than away from it.

After nine hours in the air, we finally landed in Rio. I milled around in the waiting area for several hours with the other passengers, then boarded the flight to Buenos Aires. As the plane headed out over the South Atlantic, I looked down and saw what seemed to be an endless beach extending in a narrow strip along the coast.

I was on the way to Argentina at the invitation of Mauricio Waroquiers. At the time, Mauricio was close to seventy. He had a pencil-thin moustache and the dignified look of a Spanish nobleman. I had met him several times before at macrobiotic events in Massachusetts. He was born in Buenos Aires (he is of Belgian descent) and lives in Uruguay with his wife, Patricia.

During the Seventies, Mauricio and a Dutch partner founded a large macrobiotic enterprise in Montevideo, the capital city of Uruguay. Interestingly, before macrobiotics, Mauricio's partner was one of the leading meat packers in Uruguay. Macrobiotics had turned his life around. He sold his business and invested the profits in the macrobiotic center. The enterprise grew quickly and included a restaurant, a publishing business featuring Spanish translations of macrobiotic books, and educational programs. They also appeared regularly on national television to promote macrobiotics. When his partner eventually returned to Europe, Mauricio moved the center to a resort area on the coast.

Accompanying me on the trip was Dr. Elinor Levy, a Boston University researcher who had participated in the landmark study on macrobiotics and AIDS. We were going to Buenos Aires to speak at the 1989 Pan American Conference on Macrobiotics, Holistic Medicine, and Natural Agriculture. The event was being organized by doctors and other people associated with macrobiotic centers in Argentina and Uruguay.

Mauricio and Patricia met us at the airport. We stepped outside into the bright sun. When I left Massachusetts, it was late autumn. There it was dark and cold, with long nights and short days. Here, deep within the Southern Hemisphere, we were heading straight into midsummer. The temperature was in the seventies and the sun bright and intense. It took several days to adjust to the difference.

On the way to the hotel, we reviewed the schedule. I was to give two lectures a day for the entire week. Dr. Levy would give several presentations. The opening ceremonies were taking place that night; there would only be enough time to check into the hotel before the event.

The conference was held in an auditorium in the center of the city. The outer lobby was filled with booths selling natural food, books, and other products. As I entered the hall, I saw a large darkened room with a stage at the front. Someone was at the podium speaking in Spanish. There were about three hundred people in the hall. A table sat next to the podium, with several people sitting at it. Mauricio explained that the people onstage were prominent doctors and government officials, including representatives sent by President Menem.

Mauricio guided Dr. Levy and me to the front of the auditorium. We took seats at the table onstage. Before long, the host introduced us. Maurico handed me a microphone. I stood up and walked around the table to the front of the stage. I introduced myself, not knowing whether or not my comments were going to be translated. After saying a few words, I heard a female voice from the front of the hall speaking through the public address system in Spanish. It turned out to be my translator, Miriam, who would work with me during the week.

I asked for the lights to be turned on so that people could see each other, and drew a large face on the pad onstage. I proceeded to explain how the facial features correspond to the internal organs, and how to use them to understand our health condition. After I explained each correspondence, I invited people in the audience to look at and evaluate each other. I concluded with a brief description of the macrobiotic diet and comments about how macrobiotics could unite people in the two hemispheres. As I finished, the audience erupted into applause. I sat down next to Mauricio, and noticed he was smiling broadly.

Mauricio had scheduled interviews with the press during the week. We did one radio interview that was broadcast throughout Argentina, as well as to the neighboring countries of Paraguay and Bolivia. On another occasion, we went to a television studio where I was interviewed for a nationwide program. Argentina is one of the world's leading cattle producers, and has a high per-capita consumption of beef. I stated that this was a primary cause of Argentina's high rate of colon cancer and heart disease, and that a diet of grains and vegetables could reduce these conditions. I also mentioned that cattle production is a leading cause of the destruction of the rain forests in Brazil and Central America, and stated that the macrobiotic diet was essential for both personal and planetary health.

As the week drew to a close, it was apparent that the Pan American Conference was a success. Several thousand people from throughout South America attended the lectures and other events that took place during the week. The conference also generated a great deal of publicity. I discovered that the macrobiotic, organic farming, and holistic health movements have taken root in South America and are expanding rapidly. The people I met in Buenos Aires were eager to network with other educators and organizations throughout the world. Their energy and enthusiasm convinced me that in the future, their dream of a Pan American alliance based on the principles of natural living could well become reality.

6. A Trip to Prague

The members of our group—Carry Wolf, Todd Segal, my father, and I—arrived in Prague early on Sunday morning, May 20, 1990, following an overnight train ride from southern Germany. We were met at the station by Edelgard Oelke, a macrobiotic friend who is on the staff of the German Embassy in Prague, and Dr. Ludmilla Ruskova. Dr. Ruskova is a native of Prague as well as a physician. She attended the Kushi Institute in London and is actively teaching macrobiotics in her home country.

Our first lecture in this former socialist country took place later that day in Dobruska, a small town about two hours by car from Prague near the Polish border. Upon arriving in Dobruska, we were surprised to find several hundred people waiting for us in the town hall. Earlier, Dr. Ruskova had explained that there were several macrobiotic families there who had studied with her and who had begun producing their own tempeh, tofu, and other staples and growing hard-to-get vegetables in backyard gardens.

The people of Dobruska were eager to study macrobiotics. It was apparent that they had struggled to overcome many difficulties in their practice. One of the major problems had been a lack of basic staples such as whole grains and fresh vegetables, not to mention foods like miso, tamari soy sauce, sea vegetables, and umeboshi plums. However, these and other hardships had not deterred them or dampened their energy or enthusiasm. On the contrary, their spirits were high, and they were grateful for the chance to study together.

Not only had they experienced difficulty obtaining food (under the former government they had not been able to start private enterprises such as natural food stores), but had also experienced harassment from the authorities. Contact with foreigners had been suspect, and lectures such as the one in Dobruska had been illegal.

Now all of that had changed. Prague and the rest of the country were suddenly open to new contacts and ideas. The people of Dobruska were excited and happy to have the chance to receive visitors from the U.S. and to study macrobiotics freely and in the open.

Todd and Carry had put together a wide range of sample foods for our lectures. They brought several suitcases filled with whole grains, azuki and other beans, sea vegetables, miso and tamari soy sauce, condiments, seasonings, and other staples that we had heard were hard to find in Eastern Europe. Following the lecture, these samples were arranged at the front of the auditorium, and everyone in the audience came up to see the products, many of which they had never seen before. We also presented the macrobiotic community in Dobruska with a keg of American miso donated by the South River Miso Company in Massachusetts.

Following the lecture, we went to dinner at the home of friends who had organized the event. We were served a wonderfully prepared meal that featured delicious homemade tempeh. After dinner we sang songs in English, Czech, and German and said farewell to our wonderful new friends. On the ride back to Prague, I marvelled at how rapidly the world was becoming one. Only a year earlier, it would have been difficult to imagine being served a marvelously prepared macrobiotic meal in a small village in Czechoslovakia. Macrobiotics was uniting people all over the world.

Dr. Ruskova had scheduled several activities the next day. The first was a lecture for doctors and the general public at the Motol University hospital, a leading medical center in Prague. Dr. Ruskova is on the staff of the hospital and wanted to share information about macrobiotics, diet, and health with her colleagues. The hospital amphitheater was filled with about 100 people, including about twenty doctors and hospital staff. During the lecture we discussed the evidence linking diet to cancer, heart disease, and other health problems and presented macrobiotic case histories and related research. The doctors listened intently, and the other people in the audience were grateful and enthusiastic. Across town Todd and Carry gave cooking classes for about 75 people, including many mothers and children.

Our final lecture took place in the center of Prague the next afternoon. It was held in a large auditorium that was filled to capacity. Todd and Carry both spoke to the group and thanked them for their hospitality. They mentioned that they had been deeply touched by the warmth, enthusiasm, and spirit of the Czech people. I took the podium and said that their recent social revolution had inspired the whole world and that their macrobiotic spirit would inspire many people toward a new world in the future. I mentioned that the world was indeed becoming one, that national borderlines were disappearing, and that a planetary family based on the dream of health and peace was now beginning.

Part II: Personal, Social, and Planetary Health

7. Were the Founding Fathers Macrobiotic?

The relationship between food and health is basic not only to the practice of macrobiotics, but to the traditional common sense of all cultures. We have all heard the familiar expressions, "Food is your best medicine," and "You are what you eat." Traditional wisdom such as this is a natural outgrowth of humanity's universal dietary heritage, based on whole grains and vegetables as principal foods, as practiced throughout the world for countless generations. At the same time, folk medicine, which was usually centered in the home, often consisted of simple dietary adjustments and the use of medicinal plants from the immediate environment.

Many great personalities throughout history were keenly aware of the importance of proper diet. For example, Thomas Edison once stated: "The doctor of the future will give no medicine, but will interest his patients in the care of the human frame, in diet, and in the cause and prevention of disease." Edison's thinking was completely macrobiotic in that regard.

At various times in their lives, the ideological leaders of the American Revolution, Benjamin Franklin and Thomas Jefferson, experimented with diet and practiced a semi-macrobiotic way of eating, with emphasis on whole grains and vegetables. Franklin's dietary experiments are well documented in his autobiography; the story of his arrival in Philadelphia while munching on whole wheat rolls is familiar to every student of American history.

Jefferson once wrote that he used animal food only occasionally, and only as a "condiment" to his main diet of grains and vegetables. It was their simple, wholesome diet that gave these men the strength, vitality, and clear judgement to overcome the difficulties involved in establishing a new nation. Similar examples are common in the histories of many countries.

Jefferson believed that natural agriculture, especially the cultivation of cereal grains, was vital for the future of the new country. He was particularly interested in introducing brown rice to the United States. During one of his visits to France, he noticed that rice was eaten by many as a principal food, especially during Lent, when people did not eat meat. Most of the rice eaten in France came from Italy, so Jefferson went to that country to obtain rice seed to send home to America. However, the Italian government had a law forbidding the export of rice seed. Undaunted, Jefferson risked a scandal by hiring a mule driver to cross the border into France with an illegal shipment of several large sacks of rice seed. The shipment was stopped at the border and turned back. Jefferson was so determined to introduce rice to America that he filled the large pockets of his coat with seed and carried it across the border himself.

Upon arriving in France, Jefferson sent the seed to Charleston, South Carolina where a few grains were given to a small group of farmers who then took personal charge of the planting, cultivation, and harvest of the crop. Jefferson was so pleased with the results that he arranged for rice seed to be shipped to the Carolinas from Egypt and China.

If Jefferson and Franklin could return today, they would not recognize the modern processed foods eaten so widely in America. They would probably be alarmed at the epidemic increase in degenerative disease, and by the rapid decay of society. Every day, we read of the continuing decline of modern civilization.

At the same time, however, an increasing number of people in this and other countries have shifted toward a natural, ecologically balanced way of eating in accord with traditional dietary practice throughout the world. This approach to diet and lifestyle is known as macrobiotics, and offers a fundamental method to reverse society's downward spiral and begin a new era of health, peace, and continuing development. This peaceful biological revolution is centered in the kitchen of every home. Whether or not it is successful depends on those who prepare daily food.

If Franklin or Jefferson were alive today, they would surely have grasped the significance of this new revolution, and would be champions of our efforts to recover life, liberty, and happiness not only for people in America, but for people throughout the world. These giants of human integrity and wisdom were primarily involved in shaping the political and economic constitution of a new country. The most pressing concern facing us today, two-hundred years after Franklin and Jefferson, is the founding of a new world—based on the strong biological constitution of all humanity. And this constitution, too, is being created out of the extraordinary, unique energy of whole cereal grains, the staff of life.

****

Sayings of Benjamin Franklin

To lengthen thy life, lessen thy meals.
Observe all men; thyself most.
Eat to live, and not live to eat.
Lost time is never found again.
God heals and the doctor takes the fee.
He's the best physician that knows the worthlessness of the most medicines.
An old man in a house is a good sign.
A full belly makes a full brain.
Hunger is the best pickle.

8. Crime and Diet

What is the state of our knowledge about diet and its relationship to behavior?

There is a great deal of evidence pointing toward a connection between what we eat and how we think and behave. In the Seventies, the Senate Select Committee on Nutrition and Human Needs met in Washington to consider evidence linking diet with cancer, heart disease, and other degenerative conditions. They drafted a report entitled *Dietary Goals for the United States* that was aimed at reducing the incidence of these physical health problems. *Dietary Goals* presented evidence that the modern diet is a major cause of these chronic illnesses. That same committee, which was chaired by Senators George McGovern and Robert Dole, published another report called *Nutrition and Mental Health.* They examined the connection between diet, crime, and mental health and presented a great deal of evidence to support the basic idea that diet is a major factor in thinking and behavior.

How does diet affect thinking and behavior?

The biochemical connection is important to consider. Things like blood sugar imbalances, vitamin deficiencies, and the accumulation of toxic substances such as lead and aluminum in the body lead to brain chemistry imbalances. All of these conditions are influenced by diet. Everybody knows what happens when you drink alcohol. Obviously your thinking and behavior go through immediate and noticeable changes. Food affects our thinking as well, but in a more subtle way.

One of the most common conditions affecting behavior is called hypoglycemia, or chronic low blood sugar. Because of a diet that is high in animal fats and animal proteins, the pancreas, which regulates the blood sugar level, doesn't secrete hormones properly. As a result, the blood sugar level tends to bottom out and become chronically low, and that affects our mood. Once the brain is deprived of glucose—the brain is the largest consumer of glucose in the body—in severe cases, the higher centers, the rational thinking centers, start to shut down, while the rest of the brain keeps the body functioning. So that means there's a tendency to act in a less rational way, a less controlled way, less according to conscience and more according to impulse.

Hypoglycemia also creates the desire to seek some type of food or substance, such as alcohol, drugs, or sugar, to make balance. Alcohol and drugs raise the blood sugar, as does refined sugar. Many crimes are linked to alcohol and drug abuse. These conditions are triggered by chronic hypoglycemia which is originally caused by an unbalanced diet. Studies of prison populations have revealed very high levels of hypoglycemia, as high as 85 percent in some studies, and sugar consumption among inmates is often several times higher than it is among the general population.

In macrobiotic thinking, the food we eat creates the chemistry of the blood, and that, in turn, influences the brain. The brain functions because of the nutrients supplied by the blood. If our food is improper, then our thinking and behavior will gradually change and move away from normal into what we call sickness—mental disease and crime—until proper nutrition is restored.

In the book Crime and Diet *(Japan Publications, 1987), there is an account of a macrobiotic project at a prison in Portugal. Can you comment on that?*

A group of twenty-four prisoners at the Linho prison in Portugal wanted to eat macrobiotic foods. The administration agreed and allowed teachers from the macrobiotic center in Lisbon to go there and give lectures and cooking classes. In the beginning, the prisoners were not allowed to have knives in their cells. In any case, they started to cook vegetables and other foods without cutting them. They started to eat macrobiotically and really changed remarkably. They became model prisoners and several years later, all were released. Mr. and Mrs. Kushi visited the group in prison and were impressed by their sincerity, enthusiasm, and desire to study. One of the prisoners, a former bank robber, came to Boston and studied at the Kushi Institute. After graduating, he helped establish a macrobiotic center in New Bedford, Massachusetts. He introduced many people to macrobiotics before returning to Portugal. He later married and became a father, and now teaches macrobiotics throughout Europe.

Is there an interest among people in the corrections field in the relationship between diet, behavior, and crime?

Yes, although not as widespread as the interest in diet and health that we now see among medical people. Several years ago, I was invited to speak at the annual meeting of the Correctional Association of Massachusetts. I presented studies on the relationship between diet and behavior conducted by macrobiotic people, along with an account of the Portuguese prison experiment. The presentation was well received and stimulated interest in further research. As a first step, I proposed that the cafeterias in all of the prisons in the United States live up to the suggestions put forth in *Dietary Goals for the United States*. These suggestions include reducing the intake of saturated fat, reducing the intake of sugar, cutting back on high-cholesterol foods, and moving toward complex carbohydrates like whole grains, beans, and fresh vegetables.

In the mental health field, the experiences of my friend, Stephen Harnish, M.D., are beginning to show a possible role for a naturally balanced diet in the rehabilitation of mental patients. Dr. Harnish is the director of a large mental health clinic in Manchester, New Hampshire, and works with chronically and severely mentally ill patients. In the foreword to *Crime and Diet*, he describes several patients who were helped because of dietary changes. He was able to steer them away from a traditional American diet and avoid using some of the strong tranquilizing medications that have side effects, and effect a very positive change in their lives. He told me recently that he frequently notices patients in the waiting rooms downing liters of cola, and is surprised that their bodies can take that, but not surprised that their mental faculties are not functioning well.

Could you mention several of the macrobiotic diet and behavior studies that have been conducted?

In 1981, Frank Kern, who is with the Virginia Department of Corrections and also a student at the Kushi Institute, began a three month study of diet and behavior at the Tidewater Detention Center. Kern designed the study along with Stephen Schoenthaler, a criminologist researcher. They took the sugar out of the diets of a group of delinquent boys, without the boys or staff knowing it. They were sugar-free for three months, with the following results: a 45 percent decline in formal disciplinary actions, and an 80 percent decrease in the number of boys who were constantly in trouble. The researchers felt that these results were statistically significant. That small dietary change, which is a fraction of what we are proposing, produced quite a dramatic result.

The second study was conducted in 1982 at the Lemuel Shattuck Hospital in Boston, where several graduates of the Kushi Institute had started a macrobiotic food program in the hospital cafeteria that continued for four years. Out of that came the idea to study how the macrobiotic diet could benefit psycho-geriatric patients, some of whom were institutionalized for thirty years. For eight weeks, they disguised whole grains, beans, vegetables, tofu, and other natural foods in the form of mock roast beef, mock mashed potatoes, and other dishes the patients were used to eating, so that the patients were not aware of the dietary change. There was a study group of 16 patients who received the macrobiotic diet and a control group of 18 patients who were on the usual institutional diet. In the study evaluation, there was significantly less irritability among the study group as noted by the nurses and attendants who were taking care of them. The researchers also noted significant improvements among the experimental group in apparent or manifest psychosis.

What is your impression of the Feingold Diet. It is a diet for people who are hyperactive or who have attention deficiency disorder. He rec-

51

ommended eliminating additives from the diet, such as artificial colors and flavors, and certain preservatives. He has a very specific list of things that can affect these people. Many people with hyperactive children report success with this diet. Can you comment on it?

I really appreciate Dr. Feingold's pioneering work in the area of diet and behavior (*Why Your Child is Hyperactive*, Random House, 1974). He showed that hyperactivity in children is connected to diet, and developed a dietary approach to try to solve this problem. That was in contrast to the approach of giving children drugs to sedate them. Many parents are justifiably distrustful of giving drugs to their children and turn to the Feingold diet. There was a case in New Hampshire recently in which parents refused to put their child on ritalin, the most commonly prescribed drug for hyperactivity. Dr. Feingold recommended eliminating chemical additives and refined sugar, and found that this helped in about 50 percent of the cases. However, some symptoms of hyperactivity are caused by the overconsumption of animal foods. To eliminate these symptoms, and for a more long-term solution to behavioral disorders in general, it would be necessary to also reduce or eliminate meat and other forms of animal protein.

I believe that a naturally balanced diet along the lines of macrobiotics will eventually become the key to rehabilitating social and behavioral disorders. The understanding of diet and behavior is like a second wave building behind the awareness of diet and health. In the future, prisons can become like health centers where people go to self-reflect, eat well, and study the order of nature. Macrobiotics offers not only a solution to problems of physical health, but a practical method for the betterment of society as a whole.

9. The Freedom to Teach Macrobiotics

In the spring of 1989, I travelled to a city in the United States to lecture on macrobiotics. The lectures were scheduled to take place at a local church. Several weeks before my arrival, the pastor of the church received a letter from a woman representing the local association of dietitians. Her letter implied that he had made a mistake by permitting the lecture to be scheduled at his church. Fortunately, the pastor was a good friend of the macrobiotic community and stood by his decision. Upon my return to Boston, I sent the following letter to the woman, to which I have yet to receive a reply.

Before proceeding, I think it is important to state that the manner in which you contacted the pastor of the church where my lectures were scheduled in an attempt to influence his decision to allow them to take place did little to enhance the credibility of the organization you represent. Fortunately, the pastor is a man of conscience and goodwill; upon receiving your letter he passed it along to the woman who invited me to lecture in your city. When I read your letter at the lecture, people saw it as an attempt to infringe on their right to free speech and assembly. Not one of the people at the lecture felt they had elected or in any way needed you to protect them from the information being presented.

It would have been much better had you attended the lecture and presented your objections freely and openly, rather than in the manner in which you choose to communicate. In the future, please respect the public's right to more nutrition information, not less, and the freedoms upon which this country was founded.

The tone of your letter gave me the impression that it is difficult for you to be objective about macrobiotics, regardless of the facts being presented. In any case, allow me to answer several of the questions you raised:

1. The macrobiotic diet is not a "cult." Hundreds of thousands of people in all corners of the globe practice macrobiotics knowing that it does not interfere in any way with their personal and private beliefs.

2. In my lectures I did not advocate any "stages" of diet beyond the "attractive and appealing" (your quote) standard macrobiotic diet.

3. Macrobiotic educators support, advocate, and promote adoption of dietary guidelines such as those of the U.S. Senate (*Dietary Goals for the United States*); the National Academy of Sciences (*Diet, Nutrition and Cancer*); and the U.S. Surgeon General (*The Surgeon General's Report on Diet and Health*).

4. Macrobiotics is not offered in place of nor as an alternative to qualified medical care.

I am enclosing for your consideration a book, *Doctors Look at Macrobiotics* (Japan Publications, 1988), in which ten medical doctors review the potential of the macrobiotic diet in the prevention of disease and maintenance of optimal health. I hope you will have the courage to review their comments and consider their opinions in an objective and professional manner. Please note that the doctors are themselves practicing macrobiotics and recommending it as an alternative to the modern high-fat, high-cholesterol diet.

Also, I would appreciate receiving your answers to the following questions. I would like to know your position, or that of your organization, on the following:

1. Do you support or reject the recommendations in *Dietary Goals for the United States* (U.S. Senate Select Committee on Nutrition and Human Needs, 1977)?

2. Do you support or reject the interim dietary guidelines in *Diet, Nutrition and Cancer* (National Academy of Sciences, 1982)?

3. Do you support or reject the dietary guidelines in the *Surgeon General's Report on Diet and Health* (1988)?

4. Do you agree that the modern American diet is too high in saturated fat?

5. Do you agree that most Americans would benefit by increasing their intake of whole grains and fresh vegetables?

6. What is the role of dietary fiber in health? Do you feel that Americans on the whole eat enough fiber?

7. Do you agree that unrefined, unprocessed cereal products such as whole wheat, brown rice, etc. are better nutritionally than refined and processed cereals such as white bread, white rice, etc.?

8. Do you see a relationship between diet and heart disease? If so, how does the relationship work? If not, what do you think is the primary cause of heart disease?

9. Do you see a relationship between diet and cancer? Please explain what recommendations you would make for lowering cancer risk.

10. Do you feel that organically grown foods are superior to chemically produced ones?

In the future, please make a clear distinction between macrobiotics and other legitimate and credible approaches to diet, health, and human well-being, and the so-called health "frauds" that you claim to be investigating. Also, please make a clear distinction between the broad and varied dietary recommendations that my colleagues and I are presenting and the so-called "brown rice" or "Zen" diet. Ultimately, however, whether you agree or disagree with what I have to say is not the issue. The crux of the matter is that in a free society, I have the right to express my point of view and the people of your city have the right to gather in a public forum to consider and debate whatever ideas they so choose.

10. Questions and Answers About Macrobiotics

What is a macrobiotic diet?

A macrobiotic diet is a diet based on healthy food. It includes a lot of foods that nutritionists and health authorities around the world are pretty much in consensus about: things like whole grains, organic vegetables, and tofu. And the idea is to try to minimize and avoid foods that can be hazardous to your health, like high-fat foods, highly-sugared foods, and highly chemicalized foods. Macrobiotics is actually a way of life based on the idea of living in harmony with nature. It's not a new idea; in fact, its been around for centuries. The term *makrobios* was used by Hippocrates to describe a way of living for health and longevity. We have basically revived this very old concept and brought it up to date.

How do people go about living in harmony with nature?

One of the first things we recommend people do is to look at what they eat everyday. Because, as modern nutrition and medicine are discovering, food is a key factor in health and sickness. There is plenty of evidence linking the modern high-fat, highly processed diet with heart disease, cancer, and other chronic illnesses. So as a first step, we would suggest that people begin to review how they eat and start to return to a more traditionally based diet.

Do you avoid meat?

In most circumstances, yes. I myself have not had meat in about twenty years.

The reason I ask is because some people give the public the impression that the reason they don't eat meat is simply an animal rights concern, when in fact, for many people it is quite different. You're not saying that you have a moral problem with livestock or meat?

There are ecological and environmental problems with the way the cattle industry is conducted today. There are very clear problems. And also there is an issue about the way animals are treated in the food industry, total disrespect for them as living beings. We agree with those concerns.

Am I right to say that that is a different concern than saying you shouldn't kill any animal for food?

Yes. If you're an Eskimo and you live in northern Alaska, you are not going to be able to grow cabbage. So, in order to survive, you have got to eat whale meat, seal fat, and other types of animal food. That we would say is an ecological or macrobiotic lifestyle, in that niche.

And certainly fish is part of the macrobiotic diet, at least for some.

Yes. So the ethical concern is there but it is not the overriding concern. Harmony with the environment, what works from an environmental point of view, is our primary concern.

According to the New York Times *(May, 1990) early findings from a huge study of dietary habits in China indicate that a plant-based eating plan is more likely to promote health than a meat-eating plan. Particularly the fats in meat are bad for you. Do you concur with this?*

Yes. The evidence is now overwhelming. As a result, a lot of people have stopped eating meat in the last five or ten years and have switched to low-fat foods, like fish or seafood, or high-protein soyfoods. Many people now agree that a high-meat diet is not going to benefit your health. Your risk of heart disease, colon cancer, prostate cancer, and many other illnesses increases when you eat a high-fat, high-meat diet. So that epidemiological study in China (the China Health Study), more or less confirms what many people already know, on a large scale and scientifically.

The extreme growth in the rate of heart disease is really an American and Western civilization problem, isn't it?

Definitely. When you look at Japan, the Philippines, Africa, and other parts of the world where people do not consume much animal food, their rates of heart disease are much lower than those in the United States and other developed countries. The same is true of many types of cancer. Populations with a low consumption of animal fat have much lower rates of colon, prostate, breast, and other common forms of cancer.

What about dietary supplements. Are they a part of macrobiotics?

Ultimately, our goal is to get all the nutrients we need from our daily foods. If we are eating a well balanced diet, with plenty of variety, then we don't need to supplement artificially. As a temporary measure, people eating a modern, unbalanced diet may sometimes use them. But for long-term health and well-being, we don't recommend them.

Am I correct in saying that the macrobiotic diet has some roots in Japanese diet?

It incorporates elements of traditional Japanese diet. It's not a Japanese diet, but incorporates traditional dietary practices from a variety of cultures. For example, your grandmother probably ate whole wheat bread, sauerkraut, cabbage from her garden, and ate much less animal food than we do today. Native Americans ate corn, beans, and squash, all of which are part of the macrobiotic diet. If we go back a couple of generations, people were more or less eating along the lines of macrobiotics. There were only about five or six chemicals in the food supply before World War II. Now there are several thousand. At the turn of the century, everyone was pretty much eating organic food. And if you look at their health patterns back then, you will see that heart disease was a very rare condition, believe it or not. Cancer struck one out of twenty-seven people at the turn of the century. Now it strikes one out of three. These changes correlate to the shift away from a more traditionally based diet to the modern, high-fat, highly processed diet.

What is the difference between a vegetarian diet and a macrobiotic diet?

Macrobiotics is not against the use of animal food, some animal food, depending on the circumstances. Macrobiotics is not a rigid diet. It's more like a set of principles that we can use to modify our diet based on our personal needs.

What are those principles?

The first principle is to eat along the lines of traditional dietary practice, what people did for thousands of years. If you look back, even in biblical times, whole grains and vegetables were considered the staff of life. We say respect that; it worked, it went on for thousands of years. Agriculture was self sustaining, people continued. The second principle is to change or modify your diet according to your climate. So as I said earlier, if you move up north to the polar regions, it's very ecological to eat a diet based on animal food. Whereas if you live in India, then it is ecological not to eat much animal food and to use grains and other plant foods as your main foods. We need to be flexible and adapt our eating according to where we live.

If you live in the United States, what would the macrobiotic principles for diet be?

Practically speaking, your main food would be complex carbohydrates, especially whole grains like brown rice, whole wheat, barley, oats, millet, and other high-fiber grain products. Secondary foods would be vegetables, things that you grow in your garden, things that grow in your area. The third category of food would be vegetable protein sources like tofu, tempeh, processed soy foods, whole beans, things like that. And then various supplementary foods. But your intake of animal food would be much less than what most people are eating at present. You see, animal food is now the main food in the American diet, although people are moving away from it. That dietary pattern very simply doesn't work for our personal health or for the health of the planet.

What does it do for our health?

It increases our risk of heart disease. It's well known that foods high in saturated fat and cholesterol, meaning most animal foods, will increase your risk of developing a heart attack or stroke. That's well known. In fact there was a study not too long ago. They took people off of those foods, put them on a semi-macrobiotic diet, and were able not only to lower their cholesterols, but actually reverse severe deposits of arteriosclerosis. It was a breakthrough study because it showed that heart disease could be reversed without drugs or surgery, but with diet and lifestyle alone.

Can a macrobiotic diet be of benefit to someone with an established illness?

Yes. I have worked with many people with established illnesses who were able to experience remission or recovery as a result of adopting macrobiotics. I recently helped edit a book entitled *Cancer-Free: 30 Who Triumphed Over Cancer Naturally* (Japan Publications, 1992). It features the personal stories of people from all walks of life who recovered from a variety of cancers with the help of the macrobiotic diet. A variety of other books, some of them best sellers, have been written by people with similar experiences. A good example of the way that macrobiotics can change an established health problem is the speed with which high cholesterols drop to within normal after a short time on the diet.

What do doctors and nutritionists think about macrobiotics?

There are many different opinions, just as there are many opinions about what type of approach to take for a certain illness. There is no unified consensus yet. Some doctors are eating macrobiotically. Others are eating semi-macrobiotically or going toward it. Some feel that there is not enough scientific evidence to prove that macrobiotics can help in the recovery from illness, while others recommend macrobiotics to their patients. So there is no unified approach yet. But we hope that a consensus will emerge. Because nutrition is an area of medicine that has been neglected for many years, and is only now getting the attention it deserves.

The principles of macrobiotics derive from a philosophy of life, but interestingly enough, they dovetail with the latest findings in modern nutrition, like those of the China Health Study. So a convergence is taking place between macrobiotics and the leading edge of science and nutrition. Macrobiotics, in a way, anticipated the preventive guidelines of the National Academy of Sciences, the American Heart Association, the American Cancer Society, and other public health organizations. More than thirty years ago, Michio Kushi, Herman Aihara, and other macrobiotic educators were saying that the modern diet was a primary factor in cancer and heart disease, and that a low-fat diet based around whole grains, beans, and fresh local vegetables would help prevent these illnesses.

If you eat meat only five times a week, how does that affect your health?

Well certainly it is better than ten times a week. And that is better than fifteen times. So it is a question of relativity.

I probably eat meat five times a week, usually with dinner, or if I go out to lunch. To what degree does that hurt my health?

Try to look at it this way. Think about how a hundred years ago, when people ate meat, how it was eaten. It was often cooked in a big pot with a lot of vegetables, like a stew. And the portion of meat was often quite small. Plus, they were eating high-fiber brown bread and other whole grain products along with it, together with side dishes of fresh farm and garden vegetables. Nowadays, if you go to a restaurant and order meat, practically all that comes out is a huge slab, maybe with a small salad and some French fries. That's a big problem. So if you are going to keep eating meat, that's your choice, but at least try to reduce the amount and balance it with some healthy foods.

I do a lot of running, a lot of jogging, and have a busy work schedule. Is it possible to maintain a high level of energy without supplementing my diet with meat?

The idea that you need meat for vitality is a myth, a total myth. Some of the top marathon and tri-athelon athletes in the world today are not eating meat. They are eating complex carbohydrates. Complex carbohydrates are now considered to be the best foods for stamina, endurance, and energy. As far as maintaining an active schedule, the additional stamina and energy that you get from eating well makes that much easier. With a little guidance and imagination, including cooking classes, you can adapt a healthy diet to a modern, fast paced lifestyle.

I don't have time to go to a natural foods store. Where else can I find healthy natural foods?

Many supermarkets are now selling organic vegetables, tofu, whole grain breads and pastas, and other natural foods. There are also mail order companies that will ship macrobiotic staples to your door. In the summer, look for organic produce at farmers markets and stands in your area. When you buy organic vegetables, not only do you benefit your health, you support your local organic farmers and the local ecology.

When you say organic vegetables, do you mean vegetables grown without pesticides?

Yes, chemical free.

How does that affect your health?

There is plenty of evidence linking pesticides in the food supply to cancer, to behavioral disorders in children, to all kinds of health problems. As you go up the food chain, from plant to animal foods, pesticides concentrate to a much higher degree. They concentrate especially in animal fat. If you are eating meat, eggs, and plenty of dairy food everyday, then you are getting, in addition to a lot of cholesterol and saturated fat, a pretty hefty dose of pesticide and other toxic residues. If you eat grains and other vegetable quality foods, even if they are not organic, the concentration of residues is far less. Toxic chemicals don't bind with plant tissues in the way they do with the sticky fats animal foods.

We have one of the most massive, expensive health care systems in the world and yet very little energy is put into preventing illness before it happens. Do you feel that is why more and more people are reaching out to programs like yours for dietary and lifestyle guidance, in order to prevent getting sick?

Yes. The focus of the modern health care system is not really health, it's sickness. People go to doctors when they get sick or have an emergency. But the point is, how do you prevent those things from happening? That's where macrobiotic education comes in.

Many doctors tell me they wish people would take more responsibility for their health and do the right things as far as eating the right foods and exercising. There is enough evidence showing that chronic illnesses are lifestyle related. They are not just freak accidents or things that happen for no reason. They are events that we create through our behavior, our diet, and our way of life. If we create those problems, then we have the power to prevent them from happening or to solve them if they do happen. A good example is heart disease. It's very clear that if we eat plenty of saturated fat and cholesterol, our cholesterol level is going to go up, our blood fat level is going to go up, and the deposition of fats in the arteries and blood vessels is going to continue. If we don't eat those foods, and eat a vegetable quality diet, including plenty of whole grains and fresh vegetables, those things won't happen and we can prevent that problem from occurring. It's very simple.

I have a friend whose child is developing very early. The child's pediatrician alluded to the fact that sometimes the growth hormones in animal foods can cause children to go into puberty early. Have you ever heard of this?

Yes. There was a well-known case in Puerto Rico about ten years back. In a little village, children five, six, and seven years old started to go into full puberty. Little girls started to develop breasts and boys failed to develop male characteristics. Investigators traced the problem to a local chicken processor who was using several times the legal amount of synthetic estrogen in the chicken which people in the village were eating. Growth hormones may also play a role in the increasing incidence of breast cancer, including among men. Last year, there were four thousand cases of *male* breast cancer in the United States. Incidentally, the issue of synthetic hormones in the modern food supply is well covered in John Robbins' book, *Diet for a New America*.

How do you feel about frozen and canned foods?

Whenever possible, it is better to use fresh foods. There is an intangible quality to food, the so-called "aliveness" of food, that is difficult to measure scientifically. That intangible quality is actually quite important for health. Obviously something that is freshly picked is going to have more aliveness than something that has been in a can or freezer for several weeks or months.

Are dairy products part of the macrobiotic diet?

Usually not. Dairy products are linked with a variety of health problems, from colic in infants to breast cancer in adults. Dairy foods are a major cause of allergies. The best nutrition for an infant is found in mother's milk, not cow's milk. And once that natural pattern of feeding (breast-feeding) is established, it doesn't make sense to introduce cow's milk once the baby has been weaned. Many people go directly from breast-feeding to introducing whole cereals and other vegetable quality foods.

The China Health Study came out with an interesting finding that relates to the issue of dairy products. Chinese, historically, have not used dairy products so you would think they would have high rates of osteoporosis and bone thinning because of a lack of calcium in the diet. However, the opposite is actually true. The study revealed that the Chinese have incredibly low rates of osteoporosis compared to the United States where plenty of dairy foods are eaten. So the idea that you need dairy products to prevent osteoporosis is incorrect. Studies in other parts of the world have shown that people who eat a lot of grains, vegetables, beans, and other vegetable quality foods and who consume few dairy products have the lowest rates of osteoporosis. In fact, there are studies showing that the high intake of protein involved in dairy- or meat-based diets may cause the body to lose calcium and may actually be a cause of osteoporosis.

Are there alternative sources of calcium, or is the need for calcium overblown?

No, we need calcium but there are better sources than dairy foods.

Such as?

Such as tofu, such as beans.

Tofu is in every supermarket, yet some people still don't know what it is. It's a soybean product, right? It is a bean curd.

Yes. It's quite delicious. Children love it. Children love tofu. Green leafy vegetables, the ones your grandmother told you to eat more of, are also good sources of calcium. Another good source, and I know this may sound new to some people, is seaweed (sea vegetables). Vegetables from the sea are very rich in calcium and other minerals. One type of sea vegetable that we use has fourteen times as much calcium as the same amount of milk. It's called hijiki. It's quite delicious and very nutritious. All seaweeds are incredibly rich in valuable nutrients.

I saw an interesting study recently. I don't know if it is related to what you are saying but it showed that young kids who watched the most television had the most obesity. And I'm not sure why that is.

It is completely related. One reason for that is the lack of physical activity that comes with watching television. Another is that children often snack while sitting in front of the T.V. A third reason is that most of the ads directed at children on Saturday morning television are for high-fat, highly sugared junk foods. Children who see these foods advertised on television have a tendency to want to eat them more often.

Your question raises a problem that is directly connected to diet, and that is the decline of the modern family. Problems such as divorce, separation, and family violence directly tie in with modern dietary patterns. The fact that families don't eat together any more is a major factor in family separation. In the past, parents would prepare food for their children and put a tremendous amount of love and care into their cooking. Nowadays, a T.V. dinner is popped into the microwave or the kids are hustled off to a fast food restaurant. What kind of love and care is that? I think we need to take a look at what modern eating habits are doing to family solidarity, not to mention family health.

A popular impression of macrobiotics is the image of a lot of whole wheat flour and a certain style of eating. Yet in looking at macrobiotic literature, I'm led to believe that macrobiotics offers a resolution for a wide range of problems. Why do you think the macrobiotic way of eating is at the core of solving so many disparate problems?

So many social problems are related to health. The economy is a good example. If the incidence of chronic illness continues increasing at the present rate, we are going to be in a situation where medical costs will start to consume the entire GNP. That kind of situation would bankrupt the world economy. The escalation of medical costs is a direct result of the modern decline in personal health, and that, in turn, is caused by what people are eating.

Destruction of the environment is also related to modern eating habits. The modern food system is a major contributor to the depletion of natural resources, the chemicalization of the environment, and the disruption of planetary ecology. Take for example, the problem of ozone depletion. The chemicals that destroy ozone are those used in Styrofoam containers for fast foods, as well as in air conditioners, refrigerators, and aerosol spray cans. If we eat macrobiotically, we can get by with much less air conditioning than people use today. People become addicted to air conditioning because they are eating too much animal fat, which causes the body to retain heat. At the same time, foods such as meat, eggs, dairy food, and chicken require constant refrigeration to prevent toxic spoilage. Whole grains, vegetables, dry beans, sea vegetables, and other natural foods require much less refrigeration, even during the summer.

When people eat plenty of animal food, they also desire iced drinks and foods such as ice cream to balance the excessive heat generated in their bodies, all of which require constant refrigeration. Also, people who don't eat meat usually don't need deodorant, thus eliminating the release of ozone-busting chemicals through aerosol sprays. By eating macrobiotically, you are making a direct contribution to the environment. You are also protecting yourself from environmental hazards.

Including nuclear radiation?

Yes. A delegation from the Kushi Institute recently travelled to Russia for macrobiotic activities. They met with the head of Union Chernobyl, the relief organization involved in helping victims of the Chernobyl accident. The doctors and scientists associated with Union Chernobyl were very interested in the potential of the macrobiotic diet to reduce the effects of nuclear radiation. There have been numerous studies showing that foods like miso and sea vegetables help the body discharge radioactive particles. Interestingly, when the Chernobyl accident happened in 1986, the stocks of miso and sea vegetables were cleaned off the shelves of natural food stores all over Europe. People were obviously aware of the protective effects of these foods and started eating more of them. By eating a naturally balanced diet, you can minimize the effect of environmental toxins. When your internal ecology is well balanced, you can better cope with environmental stress.

So you are saying that your body is like the planet, you have to take care of it.

Exactly. Planetary health, planetary ecology is equal to personal health and ecology. They're really the same thing.

****

From a physical point of view, human life is a phenomenon caused by the convergence of unifying natural forces and ever-changing materials. This operation must have its own rules, limitations, and duration. While it depends on the degree of power and the material, on how it is used, and other outer and inner circumstances, it can, like any physical operation, be supported or inhibited, promoted or retarded. It is possible to build rules of dietetic and medical treatment of life, in order to prolong it and create a science of its own, which we may call macrobiotics, or the art of prolonging life.

The purpose of medicine is health. The purpose of macrobiotics is long life; the devices of medicine aim at the present state or situation and its change; the devices of macrobiotics aim at the whole. We must consider practical medicine as an assistant science that teaches us how to recognize, avoid, and abolish a certain part of the enemies of life--the diseases--but that must be subordinated to the higher rules of macrobiotics.

Christoph W. Hufeland, 1796
Macrobiotics: The Art of Prolonging Human Life
trans: Gabrielle Weiland

11. The Dimensions of Counseling

Macrobiotic counseling is not limited to dietary or physical health problems. Of course, these aspects are important, but macrobiotic counseling deals with more than just the establishment of physical health. Counseling is a form of macrobiotic education, the aim of which is to guide others toward self-realization and freedom, while at the same time developing our own abilities and understanding of life. In that sense, a macrobiotic counselor is a teacher who offers guidance on life itself. Ultimately, then, macrobiotic counseling encompasses the following levels:

Self-Evaluation and Change. Self-evaluation and self-change provide the basis for helping others. Helping others begins when we help ourselves. Without self-reflection and evaluation, we cannot develop. Self-reflection enables a counselor to understand the cause of whatever problems he or she is experiencing, and to find the most effective solutions. A teacher of macrobiotics ultimately must serve as an example of macrobiotic living, not only by being healthy, but by developing such qualities as modesty, patience, humor, compassion, and a deep understanding of the human condition. As a guide for self-reflection, Michio Kushi recommends that all macrobiotic counselors refer to George Ohsawa's Seven Conditions of Health, and use them to evaluate their condition on a regular basis.

Individual Guidance. Once we begin to establish our own health and understanding, we can begin to guide others. For this

68

we need to study and understand the way that daily food affects our physical, mental, and spiritual condition. An understanding of macrobiotic health evaluation, basic anatomy and physiology, and the chakras, meridians, and other aspects of the body's invisible energy system is helpful in this regard, as a working knowledge of supplementary techniques such as massage, palm healing, and the use of special dishes, drinks, and external applications. Understanding how illness develops, and how daily food can be used to prevent it from developing, is also important.

On a psychological level, it is important for a counselor to emphasize that achieving health is the responsibility of the person himself. We can help someone take that responsibility by pointing out the cause of their problems, and by explaining how to change these causes, but the responsibility for putting this knowledge into practice rests ultimately with the person himself. In this sense, a macrobiotic counselor is an educator who helps others gain the ability to manage their health.

Macrobiotic counseling is not an end in itself, but simply the first step in a continuing process of self-discovery. A counselor inspires and encourages others to begin this process and guides them on their journey.

Family Guidance. At this level, a counselor guides families toward health and happiness, based on the understanding of the role that daily foods play in the health of each family member. For this, a counselor needs to understand the dynamics between men and women, and parents and children, how to care for children's health, and the influences that parents and ancestors have on our present condition.

It is difficult for someone to practice macrobiotics without the support of his or her immediate family. When offering individual guidance, therefore, we need to consider the influence of the home environment, and think of ways to elicit the support of the person's family.

Community Guidance. As increasing numbers of people begin to recognize the value of macrobiotics, opportunities to practice this level of guidance will arise. Community guidance necessarily takes the form of education. Cooking classes, lectures, study programs, writing, and publication fall under this category, as does setting up a business such as a macrobiotic food store or restaurant. Many people begin this level of guidance when they set up a macrobiotic center.

The principle involved in community guidance is the same as in family guidance—that is, the harmonious functioning of the group as a whole based on the health and well-being of each member. At this level, a macrobiotic teacher serves to inspire and guide large numbers of people. In the future, a network of macrobiotic educational and health centers—staffed by qualified teachers—can offer services to every neighborhood and community in the United States.

Planetary Guidance. At this level, we try to solve the problems of humanity, including war, biological and psychological degeneration, destruction of the environment, and crime, and change the underlying misconceptions that cause these problems to arise. In ancient times, before recorded history, such planetary guidance was provided by world government. Ancient world government had several primary functions: (1) to compile the yearly calendar, based on knowledge of celestial movements (including the movement of atmospheric energy through the stages of the Nine Star Ki); (2) to provide essential information about food, health, and agriculture; and (3) to establish standards of quality for basic food items such as cereal grains, water, and salt.

The macrobiotic congresses that were started in the Seventies (and which I hope are revived in the Nineties) were an attempt to practice planetary guidance and re-establish this type of government without power. The idea at that time was to begin regional congresses in Europe, North America, and other places and, after several years, to hold a World Macrobiotic Congress made up of delegates from all over the world.

At such a gathering, which should be open to all macrobiotic people anywhere in the world, delegates would present recommendations for solving problems within their respective regions, as well as global problems, from the point of view of macrobi-

70

otics. Some recommendations could be aimed at governmental agencies, medical societies, agricultural associations, and other groups, while others could be for the general public. After being reviewed and finalized by the Congress as a whole, these proposals could be presented by each delegation to the appropriate agencies and groups within their respective regions. In this way, the Congress could offer recommendations for solving large-scale social problems from the view of planetary harmony.

Spiritual Guidance. After many experiences helping others, we start to become aware of the invisible spiritual influences on human life and health. We understand that the physical world, including the human body, is a manifestation of energy, or spirit, and consider the vibrational, as well as physical, qualities of the foods that we eat and recommend for health and healing. Our recommendations may include spiritual advice, such as how to establish peace and harmony with departed ancestors and others in the spiritual world, and we may recommend practices such as meditation, chanting, and prayer in addition to diet and self-reflection. As our intuitive awareness of the spiritual world increases, so does our ability to help others.

Universal Guidance. This level of guidance encompasses all previous levels. Its purpose is to establish health, peace, happiness, and freedom on a universal scale. It includes not only those now living on earth, but all humanity—past, present, and future—on this and on other worlds. At this level, we guide people not only toward health and happiness in this life, but toward continuing happiness in the lives that follow. Our recommendations are based on understanding the process by which we have appeared on earth as human beings, and our future course once this life is complete. Along with the relief of physical, psychological, and spiritual difficulties, this type of guidance aims at establishing a spirit of one grain, ten thousand grains, or an endless appreciation for life itself.

Conclusion

The day to day practice of macrobiotics, including continual study of yin and yang, a willingness to share what you have learned, and a passionate desire to help others, provides the ba-

71

sis for developing through each of these levels. From this base, if we always seek new challenges, experiencing both success and failure, social activity and inner reflection, visible and invisible development, while keeping the spirit of humbleness and modesty, our understanding will inevitably grow. Ultimately, we become representatives of the infinite universe itself, in its ceaseless movement toward harmony and balance. This is the beginning of our life as a free human being and the goal of macrobiotic education.

****

Lao Tsu on Virtue

Cultivate Virtue in your own person,
And it becomes a genuine part of you.
Cultivate it in the family,
And it will abide.
Cultivate it in the community,
And it will live and grow.
Cultivate it in the state,
And it will flourish abundantly.
Cultivate it in the world,
And it will become universal.

How do I know about the world?
By what is within me.

Tao Teh Ching
trans: John C. H. Wu

Part III: Reflections

12. The Spirit of the Earth

Many times I have wondered about the origin of the ancient Chinese symbol of yin and yang. It is interesting that of all of the ancient symbols that portray the complementary opposites that govern the universe, the old Chinese circle is such an enigma. Yet, a solution to this problem appears from two completely opposite directions: traditional Japanese Shintoism, and a new branch of science called magnetospheric physics.

In Shintoism, there are three treasures that for thousands of years, have been stored in the shrine, or spiritual storage house. There are about sixty-thousand shrines in Japan, the most notable of which are the Grand Shrines at Ise, and shrine at Izumo on Japan's western coast. These treasures, which originate from ancient times, are the mirror, the sword, and the beads. The first two were used as reflecting devices to measure recurring changes in the position of the sun, and thus determine the arrival of the solstices and equinoxes.

The orderly progression of the seasons, highlighted by the regular appearance of the solstices and equinoxes, formed the basis of the vast cosmology of these ancient people, of which their calendar was a very useful and practical expression.

The third of these treasures, the string of beads, also served a practical purpose as a calendar. Originally, each string contained 365 beads, one for each day of the year, with special beads representing the solstices and equinoxes. These special beads were carved into a curved shape corresponding to the symbols for yin and yang in the old Chinese circle.

75

Now, why this particular shape? To answer this, we need to understand that ancient people had a different view of reality than we do. They had a clear perception of the invisible world of spirit and considered it to be a part of their daily lives. For example, they built simple shrines to honor the spirit of nature, often choosing a beautiful, natural object such as a waterfall or mountain, to worship. This is not unlike the reverence for nature found among Native American, African, and other whole-grain eating cultures. Shrines were also placed in homes to honor deceased ancestors and relatives.

Since all of nature was seen as a manifestation of spirit, or energy, it was understood that the earth itself possessed spirit. The curved beads that represent the solstices and equinoxes are shaped like the invisible field of energy surrounding the earth. When two beads are combined, we have the Chinese symbol for yin and yang. Modern scientific investigations into the nature of the earth's invisible magnetic field can help us understand this more clearly.

Until recently, it was thought that the earth had a dipolar magnetic field that extended into space. A dipolar field can be visualized as a series of concentric circular lines radiating outward equally on either side of the earth's axis. However, recent discoveries brought about as the result of satellite observation have changed this view considerably.

At the turn of the century, it was understood that the sun emits highly charged particles in the form of an ionized gas consisting of free electrons. These emissions were believed to occur periodically, and to be the cause of such things as the Aurora Borealis, or northern lights, and magnetic disturbances that occur from time to time in the upper atmosphere. However, observers soon began to speculate that these emissions do not occur in spurts, but continuously pour out from the sun, and that these charged particles create a medium that permeates interplanetary space. This resulted from speculation that the tails of comets are caused by their impact with these energetic particles.

With the advent of satellites, scientists were able to measure the earth's magnetic field. They discovered that it contains a significant number of highly charged electrons and protons, and that regions of the magnetic field close to the earth are radioactive. These radioactive regions were named the Van Allen belts. It was also discovered that the highly charged electrons and protons contained in the magnetic field originate from solar emissions, and that these emissions, which were named the solar wind, profoundly affect the shape of the magnetic field. As additional satellite data became available, the concept of a dipolar magnetic field gave way to a newer model, in which the region of the magnetic field—renamed the magnetosphere—extending toward the sun is compressed by solar wind, while the area extending away from the sun is elongated.

Recent studies have revealed that the solar wind consists mostly of ionized hydrogen (high energy protons and electrons) flowing continuously outward from the sun in a spiral pattern at speeds of between 350 to 800 kilometers per second. In general, gases that are ionized, which means that their atoms are separated into electrons and protons, are called plasmas. Plasmas are now considered to be a fourth stage of matter, and are capable of conducting electricity and generating their own electromagnetic field. The study of plasmas has produced a new branch of science called plasma physics.

Ancient people were aware of this plasmic stage of matter, and considered it as the borderline between the visible, material world and the invisible world of energy or spirit. In ancient Japan, the syllable Hi was used to signify spirit or energy. When translated, it means fire, or plasma. Ancient people also placed a symbol representing fire or spirit on their ancient calendar, called Kanagi-Guruma, signifying the application of the cyclic order of change recorded in the calendar to both the worlds of matter and spirit.

The spirit of the earth, as symbolized in the special beads and in the Chinese circle, is simply an approximation of the earth trailing its electromagnetic field as it orbits around the sun. When two of these beads were combined, the symbol for yin and yang was created. The small circles at the center of each half of the symbol represent the earth, while the surrounding fish-shaped tail shows the energy field surrounding the earth. By combining two beads, ancient people were combining into one sign the position of the earth at opposite times of the year, for example, at the spring and autumn equinoxes. This sign shows the continual cycling of the earth back and forth between opposite poles. What science calls the earth's magnetosphere, which consists of highly charged plasma contained within an invisible electromagnetic field, ancient people considered the spirit of the earth.

Science has also encountered plasmas in other areas, most notably in association with biological bodies. This study of what are now termed *bioplasmas* resulted from the development of a special technique of photography, called Kirilian photography, in which living things such as plants and animals were found to be giving off a constant stream of electrically charged energy. From the study of Kirilian photography, it seems that the human body is also surrounded by an energized, plasmic field, or aura. This is particularly interesting when we consider that both the special beads and each half of the Chinese symbol bear a strong resemblance to the curled spiral of the human embryo. In fact, when we look at an illustration of the magnetosphere, we notice that it too resembles the human form.

Perhaps in creating the beads in their particular shape, ancient people were leaving clues not only to the form of the earth's spiritual body, but to the origin of the human form as well. A similar understanding is found in the principles of Oriental medicine. The traditional medicine of the Orient is based on the idea that we posses an invisible, electromagnetic body that runs along a series of channels, or meridians. In Japan, this living energy is called ki, while in China, it is referred to as ch'i.

With the strong resemblance of the ki of the earth, or the magnetosphere, to the human form, we can speculate that the human body is a small replica of the energy body surrounding the earth. We can extend this analogy to the period of embryological development, viewing the fertilized ovum as a miniature version of the earth. Like the earth, the ovum rotates and has an electromagnetic field surrounding it. All things on earth are influenced by energy from the sun, and because of that influence, pressure from the solar wind may cause the field of energy around the ovum to assume a shape like that of the earth's magnetosphere, which, as we have seen, resembles the human form. As the ovum begins to divide and grow, as the result of nourishment received from the placenta, it develops according to this pre-existing pattern, emerging after nine months in the form of a human baby. After birth, growth continues until we achieve adult form. This stage of growth may also be guided by an invisible pattern, this time by the shape of the earth's magnetosphere itself.

Studies on the earth's magnetosphere, the solar wind, and the currents of energy contained in all life are leading science into a new frontier: the invisible world of energy or spirit. That ancient people had penetrated and understood the world of energy is clear from the symbols they have left us, enshrined simply in such things as the three treasures of Shinto and the Chinese symbol for yin and yang. Ancient people considered all things to be a manifestation of spirit, and lived accordingly. Science has developed in the opposite way, starting with matter as the basis of reality, and from there, has uncovered the world of spirit. Ours is a time of synthesis, in which these complementary approaches to life can be brought together. The meeting of ancient and modern, East and West, intuitive and analytical at the frontiers of science will enable humanity to appreciate life in its totality.

13. Spirals and Life Cycles

Everything in the universe is moving and changing. Nothing is static. There are many ways to express the universal process of change; for example, in the form of laws such as yin attracts yang and yang attracts yin; yin changes into yang and yang changes into yin. It can be presented visually in the form of circles or spirals, or expressed in terms of the sequence of stages all things pass through as they continuously change form. The five transformations, or Go-Gyo, is an example of this latter method of explanation.

In one of his many books on old Japan, Lafcadio Hearn describes his visit to a cemetery around the turn of the century. Carved into many of the markers, or sotoba, were symbols representing the five transformations, or stages of energy. An understanding of this universal cycle underlies the Hindu and Buddhist belief in reincarnation, and is one of the fundamental tenets of Oriental philosophy.

Oriental medicine is based upon an awareness of this cycle, and ancient philosopher-healers classified many things, including plants, foods, internal organs, and colors into each of these five stages. The five transformations were understood in the West. In the Gospel According to Thomas, Jesus referred to them as "five trees in paradise," and stated that whoever understood them would know eternal life.

Daily life reflects the movement of energy through this cycle. In the morning, yin, upward energy is strong. People get up and begin their daily activities, exchanging the yang, horizontal position of sleep for a yin, standing posture. Also, under the influ-

80

ence of morning energy, people leave their yang center—the home—and go out into the world. Ancient people named this stage of energy tree nature.

Expanding energy reaches a peak around noon, or mid-day, at which time it changes direction and starts to move downward. The peak of expanding energy was named fire nature. In the afternoon, we tend to become quiet and reflective, compared to feeling more active and "up" in the morning. Downward energy reaches a peak in the evening, around dinner-time, and this stage in the cycle was given the name metal nature, to convey the image of density or solidity. This more yang process continues through the evening, so that at night, downward energy causes us to exchange a yin, vertical standing or sitting position for the yang, horizontal position of sleep.

At night, our body functions become still and quiet. We receive energy from the universe, in contrast to the active discharge of energy that occurs during the day. The atmosphere tends to float between expansion and contraction, and ancient people named this stage water nature. The first rays of the morning sun appearing above the horizon trigger the movement of energy in an upward direction, and the cycle begins again.

The daily cycle is one of countless examples of the five transformations. We can chart five stages in the changing of the seasons, the monthly cycle of the moon, in the movement of energy through the human body, and throughout nature. The five transformations are simply a more detailed way of expressing the principle of change according to yin and yang. Tree and fire energy are stages of yin, expanding energy; soil, metal, and water represent different degrees of yang, contracting movement. These stages are not static elements, but transitory phases in a never-ending cycle. As an example, let us see how the five transformations can be used to understand current thinking about the life cycle of stars.

The Evolution of Stars

Over the centuries, astronomers have attempted to classify stars into groups. They have discovered that most stars (including our sun) maintain a relative degree of equilibrium, not unlike the condition of homeostasis maintained by living organisms. These more stable stars are classified into what is known as the main sequence. Stars in this group are further classified according to color and brightness, with bright blue Population I stars at one end of the spectrum, and less brilliant, red Population II stars at the other.

Astronomers have discovered that blue Population I stars tend to be located more in the peripheral regions of galaxies, while red Population II stars cluster more toward the condensed central regions. In terms of position, therefore, stars in the Population I group are yin, while stars in the Population II group are more yang. This classification is consistent with the classification of stars according to color, since blue is a yin and red a more yang color.

Stars are believed to form from clouds of electromagnetically charged dust and gas that inhabit vast regions of interstellar space. They are formed when galactic forces intersect in the middle of one of these clouds. These forces include more yang energy spiraling in from the periphery of the galaxy to the center, and more yin energy that spirals out from the center of the galaxy to the periphery. The intersection of these forces sets in motion a huge inwardly moving spiral. The gaseous cloud condenses around the center of this spiral, eventually taking the form of a proto-star. With continuing contraction (yang), pressure inside the proto-star begins to rise, as does temperature. Heat produces expansion, and this combines with centrifugal force generated by the star's rotation to slow and eventually stop the process of contraction. At this point the star stabilizes, beginning its life in the main sequence.

After billions of years in the main sequence, a star begins to decompose (yin); eventually expanding to many times its previous size, and taking the form of what is known as a red giant. These gigantic stars are sometimes several hundred-million miles in diameter, equivalent in size to the area extending from the sun to Mars.

There are a number of ideas about the fate of a star once it becomes a red giant. According to one hypothesis, the expanding star generates so much centrifugal energy that it can no longer hold on to its mass. Most of its mass flies off into space, leaving a tiny condensed star the size of the earth. These tiny stars are believed to be white-hot and are referred to as white dwarfs. If a star is very large to begin with, its final collapse may be accompanied by a sudden discharge of matter, in what is called a supernova. When this occurs, the star may momentarily discharge hundreds of millions of times more light and heat than an ordinary star.

Although many of the details are hypothetical, we can nevertheless perceive the general pattern of stellar evolution: contraction, leading to the formation of a star; followed by a state of stability; and then a phase of expansion and eventual decomposition. This process can be understood in terms of the five transformations. Condensation of the primordial gaseous cloud leading to the birth of a star corresponds to soil and metal nature; and expansion and eventual dissolution of the star to water, tree, and fire nature. The cycle begins again when the matter discharged by a decomposing star eventually begins recondensing into a new star.

Similar patterns of contraction and expansion, formation and dissolution, birth, death, and rebirth are found everywhere, from the movement of the tides to the life cycle of the stars. They represent the fundamental rhythm of life. In studying these cycles we come to terms with the essence of life itself.

14. New Science

As we saw in the previous essay, cycles of change are universal, and can be expressed in terms of the five transformations, or Go-Gyo. As Michio Kushi and other macrobiotic teachers have explained, Go-Gyo is simply a more detailed way of illustrating the stages all things pass through as they progress from a more yang or condensed phase, to a more yin, or expanded one, and back again in an endless cycle. In this article, let us see how the familiar states of matter—solid, liquid, and gas—move and change in accord with yin and yang and the five transformations.

In its most diffused, or energetic state, matter decomposes into ions, for example, hydrogen into free electrons and protons. This represents the separation (yin) of an atom into its constituent parts. This stage of matter is known as plasma, and is created when gases are heated to high temperatures. In Oriental cosmology, this more diffused and highly energized state of change is classified as Ka-Sei, or fire nature.

Upon reaching this diffused state, a process of solidification or condensation takes over and causes pre-atomic particles to come together to form atoms, and atoms to join with each other to form molecules. In this process, known as Do-Sei, or soil nature, atomic and molecular bonds become stronger, causing matter to assume a definite form.

In its least energetic state, matter exists in a solid form. Solids come in two types: more yin amorphous solids, such as glass, which display many of the properties of a highly viscous liquid; and more yang crystalline solids. In solid matter, molecular bonds are strong enough to lock the atoms and molecules of a substance into rigid alignment. In contrast to plasmas, which are composed of diffused, highly energetic, and freely moving ions, the atoms and molecules of a crystal are densely packed and have a limited range of motion. Appropriately enough, ancient people referred to this more yang, condensed state of matter as Kin-Sei, or metal nature.

When a solid is exposed to energy in the form of heat, its atoms and molecules absorb energy and vibrate rapidly. Hence, the solid melts, and changes into a liquid. The molecules of a liquid move more actively than do those of a solid, and have a freer range of motion. However, the molecules of a liquid are held together by strong forces of molecular bonding, and thus liquids have both a strongly yin and strongly yang nature. In ancient cosmology, the liquid state is referred to as Sui-Sei, or water nature.

If the molecules of a liquid are further energized, for example, through a rise in temperature, the forces of molecular attraction can be overcome, causing the substance to decompose. Here, the molecules enter a state of very rapid and random motion, and the resulting state is known as a gas. Ancient people referred to this actively expanding stage as Moku-Sei, or tree nature.

The Solid State

Of the more than 100 known elements, most exist naturally in solid form. As we have seen, there are two categories of solids:

Amorphous Solids: This more yin form of solid matter is sometimes referred to as a supercooled liquid. Amorphous solids have properties of both liquids and solids. Familiar examples include glass, tar, and some plastics. When these compounds are cooled from the liquid state, their molecules solidify in a random arrangement similar to that of a liquid. When struck with a hammer and broken, they display a curved fracture surface and do not break along definite lines. Interestingly, amorphous solids have no clearly defined melting point.

Crystals: These more yang solids have clearly defined melting points, and their constituent atoms, ions, or molecules arrange themselves in clearly defined, repeating, three-dimensional patterns called crystal or space lattices. When crystals are struck with a hammer, they break along clearly defined planes.

The arrangement of crystals in the natural world reflects the order of the universe. Just as there are seven colors in the light spectrum and seven musical tones, there are also seven possible crystal systems or arrangements.

Freezing Point/Melting Point

Under the influence of yin, lower temperatures, the molecules of a liquid begin to lose energy. This causes them to slow down, so that the bonding forces between molecules become stronger, causing them to lock into fixed positions. At this point, the liquid changes into a solid. The temperature at which a liquid becomes solid is known as the freezing point. This transformation illustrates a basic natural law: yin, or cold, produces yang; solidity and condensation.

The reverse situation occurs when we apply more yang, higher temperatures. Under the influence of heat, molecules become active and energetic, weakening the molecular bonds to the point where the crystal breaks down. At this point, a solid changes into a liquid. The temperature at which this occurs is known as the melting point. This transformation illustrates a basic law: yang, or heat, produces yin; decomposition or diffusion.

Vapor Pressure

According to the principles of macrobiotics, all phenomena are yang at the center and yin at the surface. Crystalline solids behave in accordance with this law. The molecules of a crystal are tightly packed at the center, and becoming progressively more energized and loose as they approach the surface. Some of the molecules at the surface are so energized that they break free from their lattices and pass directly into the gaseous state. The loss of atoms occurs constantly, and produces a detectable upward or outward pressure known as the vapor pressure of a solid. Because of the density of their structures, however, most crystals have low vapor pressures in comparison to liquids.

Molecular Bonding Forces

In order to better understand the nature of the solid stage, let us consider the forces that bind their molecules into crystal systems. The forces of molecular bonding illustrate the basic principle: yin (negative) attracts yang (positive), and yang (positive) attracts yin (negative). The molecules of a crystal are held together by the attraction existing between the total positive charge of one atom and the negative electrons of another.

Ionic Bonds: NaCl (salt) is an example of this type of bond. In this case, an atom of sodium gives up one of its electrons to a chlorine atom. The sodium atom then takes on a more yang, positive charge, while the atom of chlorine becomes negatively charged. These charged particles, or ions, have a strong attraction for one another, and bond to form strong crystalline molecules.

Covalent Bonds: In this case, the more yang protons of an atom share one or more yin electrons of another atom. The attraction between protons and electrons is so strong that crystals of tremendous hardness are produced. One example is carbon, which, when exposed to heat and pressure (yang), forms a diamond.

Metallic Bonds: This type of bonding is similar to the above in that it involves the sharing of electrons. However, in metallic bonding, electrons are not attached to any particular atom but roam freely from atom to atom, forming a cloud. Roaming electrons can hook up between any two atoms. The electron cloud produces several unique properties, including the ability to conduct heat and electricity. When heat is applied to one end of a metal rod, the electrons in that area speed up and collide with other particles. This occurs until the heat is transferred along the entire length of the rod.

The Liquid State

In some respects, liquids behave like gases, and in others, like solids. They are both abundant and rare in nature. Of the 103 known elements, only two—mercury and bromine—occur naturally as liquids. At the same time, however, water, the most familiar liquid of all, covers more than three-fourths of the earth's surface and makes up more than 60 percent of the human body by weight. Besides water, petroleum is the only other fluid found abundantly in nature.

Like solids, liquids are held together by strong molecular attractions, but like gases, their molecules are in a constant state of motion. Their cohesiveness is the result of molecular bonding forces such as those mentioned above, which reflect the attraction between more yang, positively charged factors and more yin, negatively charged ones. For example, hydrogen molecules are formed when the nucleus of a hydrogen atom attracts and bonds with the electron of another hydrogen atom, in a process known as covalent bonding. A molecule of water is formed when two atoms of hydrogen (yang) attract and share electrons with an oxygen atom (yin).

In another type of bonding, known as hydrogen bonding, water molecules link up to form chains. Linkage occurs when the yang, positively charged hydrogen nuclei of one molecule attract and link up with the yin electrons contained in the oxygen atom of a neighboring molecule. Water molecules are also held together by Van der Waals forces, named after a 19th century Dutch scientist. These forces create a weak electrical link between the yang oxygen nucleus of one molecule and the yin electrons in an oxygen atom of a nearby molecule.

It is the strength of the hydrogen bonds in water that create its tight cohesiveness and relatively high boiling and freezing temperatures. Water and other liquids display the following properties in accord with the movement of yin and yang:

1. Under the influence of higher temperatures (yang), the molecules of a liquid fly apart (yin), and the liquid becomes a gas.

2. Under the influence of lower temperatures (yin), the molecules of a liquid are drawn into rigid alignment (yang), and the substance becomes solid.

3. The closer the molecules of a liquid come to each other (yang), the less smoothly it will flow. This property is known as the resistance, or viscosity, of a liquid. Examples of highly viscous fluids include molasses and heavy oil.

4. Unlike gases, which are more yin, the volume of a liquid will generally remain constant regardless of whether it is poured into a small container or a large one. This more yang property is due to the mutual attraction exerted by the molecules of a liquid on one another.

5. Since liquids are more yang than gases, they have the tendency to repel pressure, a more yang factor (yang repels yang; yin repels yin). Therefore, while a gas can be compressed, a liquid will resist attempts to compress it or reduce its volume. A liquid will in turn repel pressure by transmitting it to every part of the vessel that contains it. This is the basis of the science known as *hydraulics*, a term that comes from the Greek words for "water" and "pipe."

6. Unlike solids, which generally hold a fixed shape, liquids are yin enough to assume the shape of the container they are poured into. However, if the volume of a liquid is very small, the centripetal or yang forces that hold it together cause it to assume the shape of a droplet. A more yang liquid such as mercury will more readily bead up in the form of droplets than will a more yin liquid such as water.

7. As everyone knows, liquids create the phenomenon known as wetness. For example, when water is poured onto a glass surface, it spreads over the glass like a sheet. This is due to the attractions existing between the water molecules and the molecules of the substance with which the water comes in contact. In the case of water and glass, this results from the molecular attraction existing between the more yang nuclei of the hy-

drogen atoms contained in the water molecules and the more yin oxygen atoms in the silicon dioxide surface of the glass.

Now let us consider several properties of liquids (using water as an example) that reflect the interaction between yang, downward energy (heaven's force), and yin, upward force or movement (earth's force). These two forces power countless natural cycles that reflect the movement of energy through the five transformations.

When liquids are exposed to yin, lower temperatures, they come under the influence of heaven's more yang contracting force and condense into solids. Under the influence of higher temperatures, liquids are influenced by earth's expanding energy and evaporate into a gas.

Let us now review several of the properties of liquids, using water as an example, with the interplay of these basic forces as a background.

Vaporization

In this more yin process, a liquid vanishes into a vapor and becomes a gas. It can occur slowly through evaporation, or quickly through boiling. Let us consider each in detail.

Evaporation: As with solids, the molecules at the surface of a liquid are more active and energetic than those in the central or lower regions. These energetic molecules have the tendency to separate from the body of the fluid and fly off into the surrounding atmosphere. This produces a gradual evaporation of the liquid.

Evaporation, a more yin process, is activated by yang, in the form of heat. This produces in turn, a temporary drop in the temperature of the remaining liquid as more highly energized molecules leave. A familiar example of this is the chilly feeling that we experience after coming out of an ocean or lake.

When a liquid is placed in a closed container, a state of equilibrium is reached when the number of yin molecules leaving the surface is balanced by the number of yang molecules condensing back into liquid. As with solids, pressure created by these evaporating molecules is called the vapor pressure. When the air above the liquid becomes filled with vapor to the point of equilibrium, it is said to be saturated. If no equilibrium exists, the process of evaporation will continue until all of the molecules of the liquid vanish.

Boiling: This process offers a clear illustration of the interaction between heaven and earth's forces. Heaven's force causes the atmosphere to press downward onto the surface of the liquid. Earth's expanding energy creates an opposite, upward flow of molecules into the atmosphere.

The ratio of heaven to earth's forces is about seven to one, meaning that heaven's downward energy is generally seven times stronger than earth's rising power. As a result, in order to come to a boil, liquids need the extra jolt provided by heat, which activates their molecules to the point at which their vapor pressure approaches equality with the atmospheric pressure. When vapor pressure overcomes atmospheric pressure, the liquid loses its surface tension (caused by the downward pressure of heaven's force), vapor bubbles form, and the liquid boils away.

The centrifugal force generated through boiling can be very powerful. Water expands more than 1500 times when it boils into steam, and it was the harnessing of this tremendous power that began the Industrial Revolution.

A great deal of additional energy is required to overcome the strength of the hydrogen bonds that hold water molecules together. Generally, it requires the same amount of heat (a calorie) to raise the temperature of one gram of water 1 degree C. up to the boiling point. However, upon reaching the boiling point, an additional 540 calories are required to convert the water into vapor.

At normal atmospheric pressure, water boils at 100 degrees C. However, what happens to the boiling point when the pressure is lowered? The lowering of atmospheric pressure means that heaven's downward force is lessened. Therefore, less energy is required to overcome this downward push and convert water into steam. In other words, water boils at a lower temperature.

Mountain climbers experience this when they cook foods at high altitudes. Since the temperature required to boil water is lower, food takes longer to cook at higher altitudes. On the other hand, an increase in pressure, which produces a more yang condition, increases the boiling temperature, and promotes more rapid cooking. This is the principle behind pressure cooking.

Freezing: Freezing, the process whereby a liquid changes state and becomes a solid, offers a clear illustration of the basic principle, yin (cold) produces yang (condensation or solidification). Following the application of cold, most liquids condense, and upon reaching the freezing point, assume their most dense form. At this point, the more yang, frozen sections of the liquid sink under the influence of heaven's downward force.

Water follows this same general pattern until it reaches 4 C. above the freezing point. At this temperature, it begins to expand; when it reaches 0 C. (freezing point), it begins to expand rapidly. Instead of pulling together at 4 C., the molecules of water expand at this temperature. This is due to the fact that water, a compound, contains strong polarity between its more yin oxygen and more yang hydrogen atoms. These strongly polarized atoms react in an opposite way to cold. They lose their attraction for each other and begin to separate, causing the water molecule to expand.

Ice, the product of the freezing of water, has a crystalline structure which is more open and airy than liquid water. Ice is yang (hard and compacted) on the outside and yin (open and expanded) on the inside, and since it is less dense than water, it floats. As a result, the waters of the earth continue to flow during the winter. If this did not happen, the waters in the far north and far south would freeze solid during the winter, and would block many of the ocean's currents, causing severe weather around the globe that would make it difficult for life to exist.

The Gaseous State

Gases are named after the Greek word "chaos," since their highly energetic molecules fly about seemingly without order. Gases display the following characteristics:

Expansibility (yin): Gases expand either through an increase in temperature or a decrease in pressure. Heat causes the molecules of a gas to vibrate more rapidly and therefore cover a wider area.

Compressibility (yang): Gases can be compressed through a decrease in temperature or an increase in pressure. Due to their more yin character, the molecules of a gas are widely separated, and can easily be forced closer together, or yangized.

Diffusibility (yin): Gases operate largely under the influence of the more expansive, upward force of the earth. Their highly energized molecules are in a constant state of rapid motion and tend to diffuse upward and outward.

Liquefiability (yang): All gases can be made to condense into liquid, if they are cooled and compressed. The temperature at which a gas changes into a liquid is known as its critical temperature, while critical pressure defines the amount of pressure necessary to affect this change. The molecules of a gas attract each other at close range. Lowering the temperature and increasing the pressure of a gas forces the molecules together and eventually causes the gas to change into a liquid form.

During the Middle Ages, it was discovered that the atmosphere, which is composed largely of gas, has weight. One of Galileo's associates, a man named Toricelli, invented a device that demonstrated the existence of air pressure. Toricelli filled a glass tube with mercury, and placed the open end into a dish. Some of the mercury from the tube ran into the dish, while about 30 inches were left in the tube.

Toricelli guessed that it was the pressure of the atmosphere pushing down on the mercury that caused some of it to remain in the tube. This device came to be known as a barometer, and is used today in measuring atmospheric pressure. In our terminology, the barometer works as a result of the downward push of heaven's more yang descending force on the surface of the mercury.

In France, a man named Pascal repeated Toricelli's experiment; this time with a glass tube that was 46 feet in length. Pascal confirmed that the atmospheric pressure would support a column of water 33 feet high. He also confirmed that the atmospheric pressure varied according to the altitude at which the measurement was taken. He placed a barometer on the top of a mountain in central France and discovered that the column was about 3 inches lower than at sea level.

This can be readily understood in terms of heaven's and earth's forces. Mountain ranges are generally pushed up through the activity of the earth's more yin, expanding or ascending energy. This more expansive force becomes greater the more we rise above the earth's surface. On the other hand, heaven's force, which generates atmospheric pressure, increases in strength as we approach the center of the earth. (The pressure under the ocean is far greater than at sea level, and increases with depth.)

The dynamics between these two fundamental forces—that of centripetality, or heaven's force (yang), and centrifugality, or earth's force (yin)—can help us understand all of the physical phenomena on earth. This view forms the basis of the cosmology and science of many ancient civilizations, and can be found in the traces they have left behind. Our macrobiotic studies represent the first steps toward reviving this ancient understanding and applying it as a solution to the problems of the modern world.

15. The Yin/Yang Game

A long time ago, each of us set out on our cosmic journey. We were very eager to experience this life, this earth, and had a tremendous appetite for adventure. After traveling along a huge spiral of materialization that encompasses the whole universe, we arrive at the center and take the form of a human being. When we arrive here, however, we are often disappointed by what we find. Instead of a healthy and happy world where everyone is playing freely, we find the opposite; our society, our world is very unfree and very unhappy.

When we set out from the infinite world, we established what we might call the rules of the game. In other words, we established certain rules for our amusement and enjoyment. What are these rules? They are very simple, and not complicated at all. We can learn them in several minutes. The rules of the game are nothing but endless change or movement according to yin and yang.

From infinity, the greatest expansion, we are attracted to and eventually become this tiny, condensed body. Once we reach this point, what attracts us the most? Nothing but infinity itself; the biggest yin. Everybody is actually seeking that—that is actually our play in this life, to seek infinity, and in so doing realize health, peace, and happiness. Ultimately, everyone returns to infinity, regardless of their desires or intentions.

Why did you come to Summer Conference this year? Was it to take a vacation from cooking, or to go to the party on the final evening? Each of us has a reason. However, these reasons are nothing but expressions of yin and yang. The most basic reason is that each of us felt there was something at the conference that we lacked; in some cases, health, in others, spirituality, in others, good food, because our cooking is not good yet. The polarity we felt with some aspect of the conference created an attraction that brought us here. Then, after we attract and take in whatever it was we came for, we don't want to stay any longer. We are no longer attracted and want to go home.

The same thing happens when you take a trip. Suppose you go to Europe. The reason you want to go there is because Europe is different from Nebraska, so you want to see and experience opposite things, things that are different, and after you do that for a while, you start to miss home and want to go back. The constant interplay between opposites is actually the process of life itself. In the same way, in the morning, after a night's sleep, you don't want to stay in bed; you want to get up and do Do-In, and once your body is energized, begin your daily activities. Then, after you've experienced a full day, you are no longer attracted to standing up and being active, so you lie down and sleep.

This morning you were probably hungry, so you wanted to fill yourself with food, you wanted to eat. Once you were full, you didn't want to eat more; you were repelled by food. Instead, you wanted to be active in order to discharge what you had eaten. In other words, what we call life is nothing but the constant movement back and forth between yin and yang. These permanent rules were established long ago when each of us began our cosmic journey. If we understand these simple rules we can play the game of life more freely.

How you play in this life is entirely up to you. Play can take as many forms as there are people. Some forms of play last for only a short time and cover a small space; others last much longer and cover a very wide area. In other words, the forms of play are defined by time and space, and can be classified into the following categories.

Mechanical Play: When do we play mechanically, without conscious awareness? Actually, we do this all the time. Our heart is expanding and contracting, blood is circulating, organs are expanding and contracting, impulses are traveling from your nervous system to the different parts of the body. These things take place automatically, without our being aware of them.

During the time we spent in the womb, we created our entire body out of one cell, one fertilized cell. What an incredible masterpiece! We could never duplicate that through conscious effort. The vehicle for our earthly play—our human body—is created out of one cell; but we were not aware of that creative process at all; we were not thinking, "Now it's time to make the liver, now the lungs, now the fingers." That unbelievable act of creation takes place mechanically without conscious awareness.

Mechanical responses are very immediate. For example, if I were to take hammer and shatter a piece of chalk, the chalk would respond immediately. A strong yang stimulus (the hammer) would produce an instantaneous yin response (fragmentation of the chalk). A computer works on the same principle; you press a key and there is an immediate response. Mechanical responses have a short duration, and their space is limited to the space in which the interaction itself takes place. If we play on the mechanical level, without conscious awareness, we limit ourselves to a very small playground.

Many people spend a great deal of time playing on this level. They are governed by unthinking responses such as, "Look, there's a fast-food restaurant, let's drive in and get something to eat."

People often have purely mechanical objections to macrobiotics, saying things like, "It takes too long to cook macrobiotic food; it's much easier to pop something into the microwave." Modern civilization as a whole is moving in that direction. A survey of eating habits in America found that the average man wants to spend no more than twenty minutes a day cooking; the average woman is a little better, she is willing to spend up to thirty minutes in the kitchen. Beyond that, many people don't want to be involved in preparing food, and could care less about the effects of their diet on their health.

Sensory Play: At the next level, we play with and experience our environment sensorially, like a baby does with a mobile hanging above his crib. He starts to play with it; enjoying the experience of space, distance, and color. The baby also starts playing with his fingers. He wants to explore his environment and know such things as, What is it like to feel water?, so he puts his fingers in water and experiences it directly. What an incredible experience it must have been to begin hearing, tasting, and seeing for the first time.

However, sensory play is limited to what is in front of us at the time; to what we can immediately detect through our sense organs. So, chocolate ice cream is delicious only if it comes in contact with our tastebuds. Sensory experiences have a short duration. They are short-lived and ephemeral. We experience them and then they are gone.

In Japan, the ephemerality of the sensory world is symbolized in the image of the cherry blossom. Japanese cherry trees blossom very beautifully every spring. However, their beautiful blossoms only last for a week and then fall to the ground. Yet, given the impermanence of the sensory realm, many people spend their lives seeking taste or pleasure, as if the purpose of life were to appease the senses. Sensory awareness is important, and we all play at that level, but there are much larger dimensions of experience existing beyond the senses.

Emotional Play: Emotional play involves feelings that extend far beyond our immediate sensory realm. Here we enter the realm of vibrations that can't be quantified. Feelings are subjective and unique to each person. At this level, as in all the others, yin and yang are always at work. At the emotional level, we experience opposites such as love and hate, and like and dislike; at the sensory level, hot and cold, hard and soft, pain and pleasure.

Film studios in Hollywood are making millions of dollars by exploiting these levels of play. Films stimulate the senses and emotions. Most fiction, including novels like *Gone with the Wind*, also plays on the emotions. In modern politics, winning an election depends largely on a candidate's appearance and ability to manipulate the emotions of the voters. Music is often strongly emotional; the symphonies of Beethoven are examples. Rock music is based on stimulating the senses, although in some cases, it plays on the emotions as well.

Intellectual Play: Intellectual play, or the world of ideas and concepts, comes next. This level of play is much wider. Here we work with the ability to use language, arrange symbols and concepts, and extract comprehensive ideas from our experiences. For example, when Newton saw an apple fall to the ground, he tried to figure out why that happened, and developed a theory to explain it. He extended his theory to everything in the universe; including the motion of stars and planets. Ideas cover a wider area and have a longer life than emotions or sensory experiences. However, like everything else in the universe, they are governed by yin and yang, the rules of the game, which means they are relative, not absolute, and have a beginning and an end.

Social Play: Social play is inspired by a dream or vision of an ideal society. It is based on the recognition of self and other, individuals and society. It starts with the interaction between mother and child, and expands to include relationships within the family, neighborhood, community, and ultimately the world.

Mao Tse Tung played at this level; he created an entire society. Benjamin Franklin and Thomas Jefferson also played intellectually and socially; their game was to create a new country.

Social play has a much longer duration than the levels that come before it; it can extend far beyond one lifetime. In the case of more yang social play, such as that enjoyed by Mao, someone may achieve his vision within his lifetime, after which he experiences decline. With more yin social play, such as that enjoyed by thinkers and philosophers, it takes more time for someone's vision to be achieved; however, the results last much longer.

Philosophical Play: Until we reach this stage, the direction of play is generally horizontal; starting with oneself, it extends outward horizontally until it covers the earth. At the philosophical level, our focus becomes vertical; our awareness extends far beyond the earth, and we enter a much wider playing field. Here we wonder about such basic questions as what is human life, why did we come to this earth, and what is the best way for a human being to live. When we answer these questions, we graduate to a very large scale of play.

Confucius was playing at this level, as were spiritual leaders such as Moses, Lao Tsu, Buddha, and Jesus. Yet, as far-ranging as this level of play is, it is still governed by the rules of the game, meaning that all our philosophies, teachings, and doctrines will eventually vanish and be forgotten.

Universal Play: At the next level, we begin cosmic or universal play. Our play becomes infinite, endless, and absolutely free. We are free to play on any level in this entire realm; in other words, the entire universe is within our scope. We may think that someone who is playing on this level spends all of his time fasting and meditating in the mountains. He or she may do that from time to time. At the same time, he may enjoy going to the movies or binging with friends. He is free to play on any level at any time, according to whatever his dream happens to be. At this level, we know that our play continues forever. As long as we want to continue playing, we play.

Playing Freely

One way to test your ability to play is test your degree of bodily flexibility. Children are more flexible than adults, both in body and mind, and don't want to come to a lecture like this. They are too busy playing. If children are fed properly, and given proper guidance, then throughout life they naturally develop toward the widest scope of play. This is humanity's natural course. In modern society, however, we do our best to block or interfere with this natural process. As a result, most people stop playing and give up.

When your body and mind are flexible, you can choose any role that you like; you are not boxed in. However, because of inflexibility, many people limit themselves to a narrow role, thinking, "I'm only going to play as an accountant, or as a housewife, or my role is such and such." In this way we limit ourselves. When we were children, however, we enjoyed being cops and chasing the bad guys. We also enjoyed being the bad guys. We could go back and forth, assuming a variety of roles without feeling a contradiction.

When children meet someone from another country—suppose another child—do they first ask to see his passport? Do they say, "You are from a foreign country, I can't play with you?" or "Our countries are enemies, we can't associate." No. They encourage him to join the group and play. They judge him as he is, and not because of some artificial label or distinction. Flexibility such as this is very important if our goal is to see things as they are.

The key point in being able to play freely is to keep ourselves flexible, or to restore flexibility if we have lost it. Rigidity, whether in body or mind, is an enemy of play. Mental rigidity comes from physical rigidity; from hardening of the body, the joints, and the brain. It narrows our scope, diminishes our sense of infinite wonder, and causes us to miss many opportunities for play.

Food and Play

Some foods enhance our ability to play; others reduce it. Foods that make the body hard and inflexible are especially problematic. For example, after many years of eating foods high in saturated fat, a thin layer of hard fat develops under the skin, even if we are not overweight. Incidentally, the average American today is 25 pounds overweight, and a large number of people, including many children, are obese. It is much harder to play actively when you are carrying a lot of excess around, or when it is a struggle just to move. Excess weight definitely interferes with our ability to play.

As fat accumulates under the skin, our receptivity to environmental energy starts to diminish, and our world becomes more narrow. We sense fewer possibilities for play. We are slower to respond to changes and less able to take advantage of the opportunities available to us. Foods that make the body hard and tight also produce stress. Rather than being stimulated by the challenges around us, we feel weighed down by them. The primary cause of stress is the overintake of foods that create tension in the body, especially animal foods such as eggs, meat, cheese, and chicken.

Aside from reducing the intake of animal food and basing your diet on whole grains and vegetables, keeping physically active and scrubbing your body every day with a hot towel helps melt these hardened deposits. Body scrubbing opens the pores, charges the meridians and body with energy, and re-establishes your sensitivity. You become more receptive to energy coming from the environment and from other people. It also helps dissolve stress.

Refined sugar also reduces our ability to play freely. Sugar depletes energy and weakens memory. Eating sugar makes us forget where we have come from and why we are here. Once we forget why we are here, we have difficulty creating our own goal or purpose, and usually accept a purpose formulated by someone else. Someone may say, "My goal is to make a million dollars," or "My goal is to become a corporate executive and own a condo." Originally, they may not have wanted to do these things at all, but because they forgot their purpose, they bought into a purpose designed by someone else.

In order to recall your real purpose, and design your own dream, you have to regain your memory. Avoiding sugar and eating unrefined complex carbohydrates, such as whole grains, beans, and local vegetables, strengthens memory and enhances your ability to play according to the dream that you yourself create.

Chronic fatigue also reduces our capacity for play. Hypoglycemia, or chronic low blood sugar, is a common cause of fatigue. Low blood sugar is caused by eating too much animal food, especially chicken, cheese, and eggs. Not only do these foods make us tense, they also cause the pancreas to become hard and tight, and inhibit its secretion of anti-insulin, the hormone that raises blood sugar. Because of low blood sugar, we often feel tired and fatigued, especially in the afternoon, and crave sugar, chocolate, and other sweets.

Supercooled foods and drinks, including ice cream and frozen yogurt, also deplete energy. People often feel tired during the summer, largely because of their high intake of things such as ice cream, iced water, or cold soda. When you consume super-cooled foods or drinks, your body temperature actually rises in order to make balance. If you take them continuously, you deplete your reserves of energy and become chronically tired.

The solution to these problems is actually quite simple. The first thing to do is to avoid cheese, chicken, eggs, and other heavy animal foods, all of which cause trouble in the pancreas. Secondly, base your diet around complex carbohydrates—whole grains, beans, vegetables, especially cabbage, squash, carrots, onions, and others with a naturally sweet flavor, and sea vegetables. Emphasize the naturally sweet taste of your foods, and be careful not to overuse salt and salty seasonings or to eat too many hard baked flour products. As your physical condition improves, you will have more than enough energy to pursue your dreams day after day. Eating a grain- and vegetable-based diet also helps restore flexibility to the body and mind.

The Yin/Yang Advantage

As the process of play unfolds, we play actively at each level, experiencing it fully, before we graduate and go on to the next stage. This process takes the form of a spiral that winds outward toward wider and wider dimensions. As we reach the higher levels of play, do we need to become a big philosopher with a chair at Oxford? Or do we behave like a saint or holy man? Actually, it is better to appear as an ordinary person, since in the coming age, the full scope of consciousness and play will be available to everyone. The time when everyone can realize and play on all levels is rapidly approaching. In other words, the time in which all people can play freely on the earth is about to begin.

Suppose we don't know yin and yang. Since ice cream is delicious, we may assume that play consists of eating as much of it as we can. It's easy to do. However, what is the result? Without knowing the rules of the game, we ultimately lose our ability to play. We get sick or dissolve our body. We can no longer play in this wonderful form. Therefore, whoever knows yin and yang has a tremendous advantage. Knowing the laws of the universe, we can manage our day to day life successfully, change ourselves at will, and develop the ability to play freely throughout time and space.

****

The way of life that we are presenting is a little different from that of the modern world. Instead of complexity, we offer simplicity. Abandoning the artificial, we stress the natural. Instead of the analytical, we offer the universal. Our purpose is to unite the scientific knowledge that modern man has aquired with the intutive understanding of the universe that people once enjoyed. The synthesis of these antagonistic, yet complementary ways of life can bring about a true golden age of humanity.

Michio Kushi

16. Nine Star Ki and the New Russian Revolution

Events in Moscow this past August (1991) stunned the whole world. Russian history in the twentieth century offers a clear example of the movement of energy in centripetal and centrifugal spirals, as well as the power of 9 Ki cycles to influence events.

As Michio Kushi explains in the book, *Nine Star Ki*, published by One Peaceful World Press, 9 Ki cycles occur every day, month, and year, as well as every 9 and 81 years. During each of these time periods, energy in the atmosphere cycles through different stages. Sometimes it is more active and energetic, while at others it is more quiet and still. Each of the nine numbers and stages corresponds to one of the energies of the five transformations. The numbers progress downward from 9 to 1 as follows:

9 Fire—actively expanding energy
8 Soil—condensed downward energy
7 Metal—focused inward energy
6 Metal—highly focused energy
5 Soil—balanced stable energy
4 Tree—mature upward energy
3 Tree—new upward energy
2 Soil—active downward energy
1 Water—floating energy

Each of these periods is governed by one of these energies. During periods governed by tree and fire numbers, for example, energy becomes more active and outgoing; during soil, metal, or water periods, it becomes more stable, inward, and down. The numbers can also be arranged in a square or circle with nine sections corresponding to the eight primary directions plus the center. During each of these cycles, a different number (again, moving downward from 9 to 1) occupies the center. The other eight numbers are positioned around the central number in each of the primary directions. Monthly and yearly cycles govern individual destiny, while 9- and 81-year cycles influence the broader movement of society.

The Russian Revolution of 1917 occurred during an 81-year cycle in which the energy of 1 Water occupied the center. During that period, which lasted from 1874 to 1955, 5 Soil was in the south, a position of high energy and activity. Five Soil concentrates energy and power toward the center. It is the number of government and control.

Because that period was governed by the energy of 1 Water, which corresponds to the energy of deep winter, and because the number 5 was in an active position, a more yang, centripetal social spiral went into effect. The movement of energy in a yang direction enabled Lenin's Bolshevik Party to seize control over vast territories and diverse populations, forging them into the entity that became the Soviet Union. In the Russian Revolution of 1991, however, energy is moving in the opposite direction. In this yin spiral, nationalism, self-determination, and independence created powerful centrifugal forces that caused the yang center to collapse.

This spiral began when a new 81-year cycle took effect in 1955. This new cycle is governed by the strongly expansive, and potentially explosive energy of 9 Fire, which is similar to the energy of full summer. (Nine fire follows 1 Water in the cycle.) The 9 Fire cycle will last from 1955 to 2036. In this new arrangement of numbers, 5 Soil moved to the north, a position opposite to its position during the previous cycle. North is the position of inactivity and dormancy, corresponding to the energy of deep winter. As a result, power that had spiraled into the center during the previous cycle began to spiral outward in the opposite direction. Thus the Soviet Union could no longer maintain strong central control and came apart.

The new Russian Revolution took place in 1991, a 9 Fire year during which centrifugal force has been especially strong (compounded by unusually hot and dry weather this summer.) The month of August, in which these events took place, was an 8 Soil month. The energy of 8 Soil corresponds to early morning just before dawn, the time when night changes into day. It is the energy of change or revolution, so it was predictable that revolutionary developments would occur during this time.

Because of its northern location, events in Russia may not become as explosive as those in Yugoslavia, where a similar spiral of decomposition is occurring. Yugoslavia is closer to the strong expansive energy of the equator, and this increases the amount of centrifugal force governing events.

The tendency toward rapid change and decomposition will accelerate as we move further into the 9 Fire cycle. Degenerative disease, mental illness, and environmental destruction are all part of this trend, as is the breakdown of established order. The danger here is that centrifugal force will cause events to spiral out of control. For example, one of the most urgent concerns in regard to the breakup of the Soviet Union is who will assume control over its nuclear arsenal. The strong centrifugal tendency of the present age could result in these weapons being channeled to other countries, and to a loss of control over them.

To pass through these difficult times, we need the strong binding power of well-prepared natural food, especially that provided by whole grains, beans, local vegetables, and other foods rich in complex carbohydrates. It is essential that we master the appropriate use of fire in cooking to counterbalance the misuse of fire in modern technology. The macrobiotic way of life, which begins from proper cooking and diet, is the most essential means for passing through the coming era and beginning a new world.

Sources

1. John and Yoko in Boston
This chapter is from personal notes.
2. Dietary Goals for the United States
This chapter is from personal notes.
3. Images of Japan
This chapter is from letters sent to students at the Kushi Institute, Boston from October, 1978 to May, 1979.
4. How *Recalled By Life* Happened
This chapter is from personal notes.
5. Buenos Aires
This chapter is from personal notes.
6. A Trip to Prague
This chapter is based on an article entitled, *Macrobiotics in Czechoslovakia,* published in *The One Peaceful World Newsletter,* Becket, Mass., Summer, 1990.
7. Were the Founding Fathers Macrobiotic?
This chapter is from an article entitled, *Were the Founding Fathers Macrobiotic?* published in the *World Macrobiotic Society Newsletter,* East West Foundation, Boston, Mass., 1980.
8. Crime and Diet
This chapter is based on an interview entitled, *Crime and Diet,* published in *Macrobiotics Today,* Oroville, Ca., January/February, 1992.
9. The Freedom to Teach Macrobiotics
This chapter is from personal correspondence.
10. Questions and Answers About Macrobiotics
This chapter is based on an interview published in *MacroNews,* Phila., Pa., Winter, 1991 and Spring, 1992.
11. The Dimensions of Counseling
This chapter is based on an article entitled, *The Dimensions of Macrobiotic Counseling,* published in *Macrobiotics Today,* Oroville, Ca., May/June, 1992.
12. The Spirit of the Earth

This chapter is based on an article entitled, *Yin/Yang and the Spirit of Earth*, published in *Order of the Universe*, Boston, Mass., 1977.
13. Spirals and Life Cycles
This chapter is based on material published in the booklet, *Science and the Order of the Universe.*, Boston, Mass., 1980.
14. New Science
This chapter is based on material published in the booklet, *Science and the Order of the Universe*, Volume Two, Boston, Mass., 1980.
15. The Yin/Yang Game
This chapter is from a lecture at the Kushi Foundation Macrobiotic Summer Conference in Great Barrington, Mass., 1988.
16. Nine Star Ki and the New Russian Revolution
This chapter is based on an article entitled, *The New Russian Revolution: A Nine Star Ki Observation*, published in *MacroNews*, Phila., Pa., Fall 1991.

****

Of Related Interest

By Edward Esko
Healing Planet Earth

By Edward and Wendy Esko
Macrobiotic Cooking for Everyone

By Michio Kushi and Edward Esko
Other Dimensions
The Macrobiotic Approach to Cancer
Nine Star Ki
Forgotten Worlds
The Holistic Health Book

Edited by Edward Esko
Crime and Diet
Doctors Look at Macrobiotics
Cancer and Heart Disease

Bibliography

Books

1. *The Book of Macrobiotics*. Michio Kushi with Alex Jack. Japan Publications, 1986.
2. *One Peaceful World*. Michio Kushi with Alex Jack. St. Martin's Press, 1986.
3. *Other Dimensions: Exploring the Unexplained*. Michio Kushi with Edward Esko. Avery, 1991.
4. *Food Governs Your Destiny*. Michio and Aveline Kushi, with Alex Jack. Japan Publications, 1991.
5. *The Cancer-Prevention Diet*. Michio Kushi with Alex Jack. St. Martin's Press, 1983.
6. *Diet for a Strong Heart*. Michio Kushi with Alex Jack. St. Martin's Press, 1985.
7. *The Book of Do In*. Michio Kushi. Japan Publications, 1979.
8. *Cancer-Free: 30 Who Triumphed Over Cancer Naturally*. East West Foundation, with Ann Fawcett and Cynthia Smith. Japan Publications, 1992.
9. *Recovery: From Cancer to Health through Macrobiotics*. Elaine Nussbaum. Japan Publications, 1986.
10. *Macrobiotics and Oriental Medicine*. Michio Kushi with Phillip Janetta. Japan Publications, 1991.
11. *Natural Healing through Macrobiotics*. Michio Kushi, with Edward Esko and Marc Van Cauwenberghe, M.D. Japan Publications, 1979.

12. *The Macrobiotic Approach to Cancer*. Michio Kushi, with Edward Esko. Avery, 1991.

13. *Macrobiotic Home Remedies*. Michio Kushi, with Marc Van Cauwenberghe, M.D. Japan Publications, 1985.

14. *Macrobiotic Diet*. Micho and Aveline Kushi, with Alex Jack. Japan Publications, 1985.

15. *AIDS, Macrobiotics, and Natural Immunity*. Michio Kushi, with Martha Cotrell, M.D. Japan Publications, 1990.

16. *Standard Macrobiotic Diet*. Michio Kushi. One Peaceful World Press, 1991.

17. *Nine Star Ki*. Michio Kushi, with Edward Esko. One Peaceful World Press, 1991.

18. *Let Food Be Thy Medicine*. Alex Jack. One Peaceful World Press, 1991.

19. *The Macrobiotic Way*. Michio Kushi. Avery, 1985.

20. *Macrobiotic Palm Healing*. Michio Kushi, with Olivia Oredson. Japan Publications, 1989.

21. *Promenade Home: Macrobiotics and Women's Health*. Gale and Alex Jack. Japan Publications, 1988.

22. *How to See Your Health*. Michio Kushi. Japan Publications, 1980.

23. *Your Face Never Lies*. Michio Kushi. Avery, 1983.

24. *Making the Transition to a Macrobiotic Diet*. Caroline Heidenry. Avery, 1988.

25. *Healing Planet Earth* by Edward Esko, One Peaceful World Press, 1992.

Periodicals

One Peaceful World, Becket, MA
Macro News, Philadelphia, PA
Macrobiotics Today, Oroville, CA

About the Author

Edward Esko was born in Philadelphia on October 16, 1950. He began macrobiotic studies with Michio Kushi in 1971 and for nearly twenty years has taught macrobiotic philosophy throughout the United States and Canada, as well as in Western and Eastern Europe, South America, and Japan.

He has lectured on modern health issues at the United Nations in New York and is on the faculty of the Kushi Institute of the Berkshires. He is the author of *Healing Planet Earth* (One Peaceful World Press, 1992) and has co-authored or edited several popular books, including *Natural Healing through Macrobiotics*, *Other Dimensions*, and *Nine Star Ki*. He lives with his wife, Wendy, who is also a teacher of macrobiotics, and their seven children in Becket, Massachusetts. Edward lectures regularly at the Macrobiotic Residential Seminar in Becket, and in the Kushi Institute's Leadership Studies Program. Information on his lecture schedule can be obtained from the Kushi Institute, Box 7, Becket, MA 01223, (413) 623-5741.